This
Cybernetic
World

*V. L. Parsegian came to the
United States during World
War I as a very young
refugee from his native
(Turkish) Armenia. He
studied at M.I.T. and, while
engaged in industrial research
in 1948, he received his
Ph.D. in nuclear physics from
New York University. He
later served as Director of the
Research Division of the New
York Operations Office of the
Atomic Energy Commission.*

*Since 1954 Dr. Parsegian has
been associated with the
Rensselaer Polytechnic Institute.
He served first as Dean of the
School of Engineering until
1961, when he was appointed
to the distinguished Chair of
Rensselaer Professor. Dr.
Parsegian is the author of
numerous books and articles
and is currently developing
new teaching materials that
involve the interrelationship
of science, technology, the
humanities, and the fine arts.*

This Cybernetic World OF MEN MACHINES AND EARTH SYSTEMS

BY V. L. PARSEGIAN

1972
DOUBLEDAY & COMPANY, INC.
GARDEN CITY, NEW YORK

Library of Congress
Catalog Card Number 71–175393
Copyright © 1972 by V. L. Parsegian
All Rights Reserved
Printed in the United States of America
First Edition

To Varsenig

Preface

Whether one attends conferences of biologists, of social scientists, of economists, or of other professional groups, or is exposed to the more serious talk of the cocktail hour, the words *systems* and *cybernetics* are likely to crop up. An enthusiastic youngster shining my shoes on the Atlantic City boardwalk threw the word cybernetics at me to prove his awareness of the modern world. Those who use the words most freely may not always have the best understanding of the subject. Nevertheless the frequent occurrence of the term reflects a range of applicability and significance that has yet to be probed to its fullest depth and scope.

Professional interests in systems and cybernetics now encompass a wide range of disciplines and activities, including some that appear to be only distantly related to each other. This gives the field a multidisciplinary character that is like a breath of fresh air in a world that is too specialized for its own good. As proposed by its founder, Norbert Wiener, *cybernetics is the science of control and of information, whether applied to the living world or to the inanimate machine*. It has come to represent a quite general *search for relationships* among phenomena. Some people distinguish the term cybernetics from what is called *general systems theory,* but all too often the distinctions seem to be more superficial than real.

In their most elementary form the principles of cybernetics may be applied to mechanisms that regulate the speed of rotation of an engine or control the temperature of a room. The principles apply as readily to the muscular movements of the body. Control systems require suitable *feedback,* which in refined form has the quality of *information* as one might find it in a computer or in connection with the nervous system. Some cyberneticists concern themselves solely with neurological processes, while others search for comparable capabilities for learning, memory, and recall in the electronic computer. For others the principles find fresh meaning when dealing with social situations or when dealing with the specter of over-powering population increases and pollution crises.

In a more philosophical vein, control implies the existence of a goal or purpose, or *orderliness*. Does the cybernetic approach there-fore offer a framework for pursuing the larger questions of the origin of life, of evolutionary processes, or of the "purposes" and end goals of natural processes? These topics and questions are explored in this volume, without, however, suggesting final answers.

The writing of this book follows completion of a six-year project that developed textbooks for a new *Introduction to Natural Science*. Designed for non-science and science majors alike, the new texts integrate the physical and life sciences, with due attention to the philosophical, historical and social implications of modern science. It was during the preparatory stages of that project that I invited the participation of Professor Wiener, whose contributions would have been considerable had he lived. "I am with you in spirit," he wrote from Holland only some days before he died, and indeed the concepts of systems and cybernetics play major roles in the new course because of the relationships they reveal among phenomena in the physical and life sciences. As one student declared after she was exposed to the systems theme, "I cannot look at anything with-out looking to see what factors bear on the situation and how they are related."

Most publications on cybernetics that followed Professor Wiener's beautiful exposition have tended to emphasize highly specialized aspects of the field. The present volume is designed to present a broader view of the subject, to be read by laymen as well as by professionals, since there is no need to hide the common sense and beauty of the subject behind equations. My hope is that readers will find the treatment understandable and sufficiently exciting to encourage the use of the "cybernetic approach," whatever that may turn out to be, for their own way of life and thought.

I am indebted to Academic Press for permission to utilize a number of illustrations as well as some portions of text material from the *Introduction to Natural Science*.

                                                                    The Author

Contents

Illustrations

This
Cybernetic
World

CHAPTER 1

Origins and Concepts
of Cybernetics

"The cybernetics of men, as you, Socrates,
often call politics . . ."*

Plato (428–348 B.C.)

At the Cybernetics Research Institute in Washington, D.C., where
training facilities are combined with laboratory research, a little
girl and a returning veteran are being fitted with simple mechanical
gadgets designed to take the place of arms that were lost through
accident and through war. In a large laboratory a computer system
costing several millions of dollars is exploring approaches whereby
the thousands of influences that determine the life and death of a
community can be understood for what they are doing to a particular
metropolitan center. At a distant military station the guns that
stand guard are controlled by complex electromechanical mechanisms
that are ready to follow on the heels of any incoming enemy
planes. In a university field station scientists are studying the living
habits of animals and birds and the effects of insecticides on ecological balances. The people who operate in each of these environments may be as different in personality and attitudes as the
objectives of their operations seem to be. They nevertheless have
in common certain principles in the way they go about their tasks,
the common denominator being their utilization of the concepts and
approaches of *cybernetics*.

What are the common features? To begin with, each of the
situations involves variables. Each involves *interactions* of machines
or organisms *with the environment*, the interactions often taking
circuitous routes. Each involves an element of *purpose*, or objective,

* From Plato's *Clitophon*

and utilizes *control principles* addressed to those purposes. The interactions involve *feedback,* wherein the results of any act are fed back to modify the initial act. The feedback may take the form of *information.* Moreover, each represents a dynamic situation in which *energy* is utilized to respond to changes and yet *to maintain stability* of sorts. In fact the utilization and control of energy constitutes a main interest of cybernetics whether the energy is mechanical or human.

The quotation that begins this chapter suggests that the principles of cybernetics reach beyond gadgets and equipment and apply to the subtler features of human interests as well. Indeed the psychiatrist who searches for childhood causes of instability against the mores (controls) of society is a cyberneticist of sorts without necessarily admitting to the title. The generation of parents who puzzle over what brought about the current youth rebellion would do well to wonder in terms of the subtleties of feedback influences that transform curses to blessings and blessings to curses.

The cybernetic approach

The approach of cybernetics differs significantly from the more conventional methods of science. Progress in the physical and biological sciences has been due in large part to what is generally called the *reductionist* approach, whereby a complex phenomenon is studied by analyzing its parts or elements. For example, in the case of a bicycle the essential features would be derived from analysis of the wheels and other parts that make up the whole unit. The human body also is best studied by reducing focus to the individual parts, organs, and processes that make up the body. In the end, however, one has to view the body as an organismic, functioning, thinking, talking "whole" in order to gain a meaningful picture of what constitutes a human being. And even newer, unexpected functions come into play when the human body mounts the bicycle to ride it. In other words, when the "whole" is reduced to its parts the qualities of the "whole" are likely to disappear. As the physicist Werner Heisenberg expressed it, "It is impossible to explain qualities of matter except by tracing them back to the behavior of entities which themselves no longer possess these qualities." The science of cybernetics nevertheless tries to emphasize "the whole" as a *system* while also examining the elements and the interrelationships that give the system its special characteristics.

There is another interesting feature of the cybernetic approach. The practice of tit for tat had its origin in natural processes long before Newton gave it more-formal analysis in terms of action-reaction principles and before mighty nations adopted it as a cardinal rule for their foreign policy. Ancient justice, from which we have departed too little, demanded retribution in terms of "an eye for an eye and a tooth for a tooth." The Christian admonition of two thousand years ago to return good for evil failed to make impact in the intervening centuries and still appears somewhat out of human reach. Of late, however, there has developed awareness that an evildoer (and society) may gain much more from medical help than from a stay in jail. We have also come to realize that in many real-life situations the reaction, or feedback, from an action may return by circuitous paths and with unexpected effects. One can quote many examples from the field of economics, from experiences of war and peace, and from personal experiences involving tragedy that brought deeper values; or "good fortune" that boomeranged with less-pleasant results. These are among the situations, involving feedback influences of many kinds, that concern the science of cybernetics.

The scope of cybernetics

It is not overly bold to state that the application of the concepts and approach of systems and cybernetics is likely to improve one's understanding of any situation that is overburdened with contradictions, whether it is in the behavioral, economic, or technical realm. The reason is that the appearance of contradictions is in truth largely due to failure to understand *relationships,* and more than anything else, *cybernetics aids in the study of relationships.* To be sure, the occasions have been relatively few when cybernetics has given complete or even adequate answers to specific problems; nevertheless the occasions have been just as rare when the effort did not prove of value for the information that it did reveal.

What makes the application of the principles of systems and cybernetics so attractive? To begin with, the formalized concepts of cybernetics have emerged from several decades of down-to-earth experience involving control of industrial and other processes. One of these decades coincided with the Second World War and included some rather sophisticated research on systems that combined servomechanisms, computers, human beings, and the exigencies of war. The latter conditions made it especially necessary to pull together the full human and material resources of the allies to win the war. Never before had projects brought together such varieties of skills of industrialists, scientists, engineers, and behavioral and medical scientists to work toward new ways of achieving the common goal.

The war finally ended, but the relationships of skills and interests fortunately did not fall asunder. There were a few individuals who, through the encouragement and genius of Norbert Wiener, sought new fruits from this confluence of disciplinary interests. Among other activities, the tasks in which they had been engaged involved servomechanism systems for control of gunfire. They now engaged in discussions that became breeding ground involving the overlapping of three rather different areas. One was the theory of communication, to which there had been notable contributions by C. E. Shannon.* The second field was neurophysiology, wherein the work of Warren McCulloch* and others promoted a more careful analysis of the similarities and contrasts between neural and especially brain functions and computer and mechanical control functions. The third was the sudden emergence of computers that were larger and more versatile instruments for dealing with problems involving many variables and experiences.

Even more important than the skills was the *attitude* of the individuals engaged in this search for scientific approaches relatively unfettered by the weaknesses of overspecialization but retaining the values of specialization. Nor should we underestimate the importance of the social and political framework that contributed to the promotion of cybernetics, namely the increasing complexity of modern life. This complexity had brought greater awareness that the research problems of the physical and biological sciences, and problems generated by the products of the sciences having implications for war and peace, ecology, food, health, disease, and national economics, demanded co-operative effort on the part of the people involved. Not the least of the factors was the feeling among

* See References.

scientists of frustration and disgust with the end results of the war, a feeling that motivated a search for methods that might offer more-effective solutions to the problems of human societies and of political conflict. For instead of peace the end of the war brought conditions that threatened even greater conflicts and the fearful holocaust of nuclear war at the hands of the scientists themselves.

It will be useful to go even further into history for the background of these developments.

The ancient roots of cybernetics

The quotation from Plato that introduces this chapter will be surprising indeed to most people, since it is customary to think of cybernetics as a new science. But as is so often true, the ideas and issues we struggle with today had beginnings and modest roots in the ancient Chinese, Indian, Sumerian, Babylonian, Egyptian, Hittite, Hebrew, and more often the Greek civilizations. The technology of their periods fashioned ceramics and metal products and constructed huge edifices and memorials. Control was necessary for performing all these activities, control that was more often the skill of hand and eye than of mechanical gadgets. Their accomplishments in turn had older roots in sharp stones, clubs, the bow and arrow, and in the wedge and the wheel. As the brain became more "agile" and sophisticated with each new tool, the Neolithic period (around 8000 B.C.) introduced agriculture, animal husbandry, houses of sun-baked brick, and millstones for grinding grain into flour. The "tools" became extended into such areas as religious worship, medicine, and astrology, the interest probably being cultivated at least in part by the idea of man's controlling his own fate. Then came the Bronze Age, the pyramids, and the Iron Age.

We do not know when man first found himself afloat on a raft, or when he fashioned the first boat and oar. Nor do we know when it was found possible to steer a ship by use of rudderlike additions. We can be sure, however, that the Phoenician navigators must have developed considerable know-how in the art of navigation and steering of ships by a combination of human skill and mechanical contrivances. Thus in the centuries that followed until the period of the early Greek philosophers, the concept of control (by steering) was well developed. *Kybernes* was the Greek term for *steersman,* the same word that gave root to the Latin *gubernator* for *steersman* and to our current word *governor.* Current use of the word *governor* may equally refer to a mechanical gadget that controls the speed of a steam engine or to the presiding official of state government or even to one who in some situation maintains control over the fortunes and thoughts of other people. The spelling of the word has changed, but the underlying concepts of the term seem to be the same as those that motivated Plato and his peers and that motivated Norbert Wiener to name the new science *cybernetics.*

The Industrial Revolution

During the Greek period the trend was to separate philosophy and science from technology. As a result the art of control found little progress. The same separation continued through the centuries that followed. Truth and knowledge remained identified with the Church, and only rarely were they differentiated from Church doctrine. In its most attractive form, the spirit of the times was expressed by Thomas Aquinas (1225–74), who preached that the *purpose** of man's very existence was the opportunity it afforded to live the good life. This outlook was on its way out at the time of Francis Bacon (1561–1626) and of Galileo (1564–1642), and was obsolete at the time of Isaac Newton in the late 1600s. Interest had become strong in the movements of heavenly bodies and of smaller objects. Experiments and new concepts began to alter age-old theories at the hands of men such as Copernicus, Galileo, Kepler, and Newton. The three laws of Newton, to which we shall refer in Chapter 3, spelled out basic principles governing behavior of material objects. The principle that every effect had a cause became firmly established for mechanical situations. When, a little later, the steam engine was invented and could serve as a power unit, machines were ready to take advantage of new possibilities for relieving man of many burdensome tasks and for mass production of goods.

The spirit of the times reached for rationalism in other areas. Minds that had suddenly discovered the rules for cause-and-effect relationships in the mechanical features of their environment could

---

* As we shall see presently, the element of "goal-seeking," or "purpose," is often present in a "cybernetic system."

not avoid looking for such relationships in other areas as well. So it was that early in the eighteenth century there emerged the age of reason (or rationalism), which touched all aspects of life— scientific, technological, religious, political, and social. The science of mechanics had found reasonably firm footing. From the ideas of thermodynamics and chemistry emerged new applications before there was even primitive understanding of the mechanisms involved in those areas. The interests of many investigators were directed toward applied science, i.e., technology. Trade and commerce, which had expanded during the seventeenth century, looked to machines for new products for trade and profit. Some historians claim that the new Protestant ethic contributed to the development of technology and science, and that a Puritan, non-conformist religious spirit in England had already made technical progress and the pursuit of useful work a prime objective of life. The preaching of John Wesley, who founded Methodism, or of John Calvin, reached every man with a message that demanded hard work along with rugged faith. The concept of a free-enterprise economic system in England gave impetus to inventions that promoted production, trade, and profit. The rise of commerce helped to "free" the peasant from the land. Propertyless peasants flocked to the cities to find work, thereby contributing to the rise of the factory system of production. In time there developed more interest in labor-saving devices to reduce costs. The use of coke in blast furnaces improved metallurgical processes and made possible new kinds of steel with which to build better machines for the textile industry. Production of sulfuric acid and of sodium carbonate on a large scale in the second half of the eighteenth century promoted faster progress in chemical industries. By the end of that century, the Industrial Revolution was well along in England, although on the Continent there was greater dependence on the government and on the guild system.

The Puritan spirit also existed in the colonies of England, especially in what were to become the United States of America. Benjamin Franklin was a scientist-statesman (although certainly no Puritan) whose comprehension encompassed the values that lay in a combination of progressive science and technology, shrewd economics, and national progress. His admonition to young men to "waste neither *time* nor *money*" represented the spirit of the Industrial Revolution.

Energy and modern civilization

Among the factors that permitted rapid social change was the utilization of energy derived from both natural and human resources. The Industrial Revolution was much more than simply an extension of applied science into production plants. It brought industrialists and commercial people into the ruling circles. The factories, with their new forms of servitude, became breeding grounds for social upheaval, which spread from England and the Continent to the New World. There seemed to be in these developments the elements of new hopes and new means for achieving a social revolution that might free the common man from want and virtual slavery. Factories required skilled labor, which in turn demanded a higher level of education for many more people in order to design and care for the machines. There was demand for a wider variety of educational preparation as well, including instruction in technology. The first institution of higher education devoted to science and technology—the École Polytechnique—was established in Paris in 1794–95 to meet the military needs of France.* Military needs were then, as they always had been and continue to be to this day, patrons of technological progress.

There was a very solid "mechanical" base that aided this vigorous period of history, namely the invention of machines that were capable of utilizing energy sources with greater effectiveness. Energy exists in many forms: kinetic, potential, mechanical, electrical, chemical, thermal, and radiant energy, and may be transformed from any one form to other forms with varying degrees of efficiency. As long as man had only another man or an animal to pull the plow, to grind wheat, or to pull wagons, his economy could not change too much from that of the early Egyptians. But when the steam engine was invented, when coal could be mined with the help of steam power, and the economy could shift from the individual producer or guild system to power production methods, the In-

* In the United States, involvement in technology on the part of schools of higher education began in the Hudson River Valley. The military aspects were begun at West Point in the early 1800s, perhaps by 1817, under Sylvanus Thayer. The earliest formal non-military program in civil engineering was established in 1835 at Rensselaer Polytechnic Institute, Troy, New York, founded in 1824 with that end in view.

dustrial Revolution could scarcely be prevented. With steam power came larger factories and the railroads, the latter proving to be a special boon for the expansion of the American colonies into the great West.

Before long, experiments with electricity, electric generators, and motors demonstrated that electric energy offered variations and advantages. Electric energy offered advantages both for powering small and large machinery and for feeding vast networks of distribution lines throughout the civilized world. There came internal-combustion engines, discovery of large oil deposits, and refineries for conversion of crude oil to gasoline. New fuels, "horseless carriages," and new production methods all followed apace to reach the highly sophisticated stage of the twentieth century.

It is interesting to compare the energy consumption of various civilizations. Some of the earliest societies appear to have made such extensive use of fire as to account for the deforestation of large areas of Africa. Apparently even in the hot climates of Africa there was need to keep fires burning for protection from animals. But generally, in very early societies energy-consumption levels remained low and limited to cooking, warmth, and protection from animals. When mining, smelting, and forging operations became common in the Babylonian and Greek periods, there developed some industrial use of fuel, largely wood. The shift to coal in the seventeenth century, then to oil, water power, and now nuclear power has continued to increase energy utilization with each year. (Unfortunately, nearly all energy sources used in the United States are of the kind that cannot be restored again in our time—namely, coal, oil, and natural gas deposits.)

Ironically we have arrived at a decade of history when the prodigal use of energy and of material resources threatens to be the undoing of the high standard of living that came about through control of energy. Indeed the situation has reached crisis proportions in communities around the world, where power stations and combustion engines spew sulfur and carbon compounds and particulate matter into the atmosphere to foul the air, and chemical plants consume energy and spew wastes that reduce fish life and make fresh waters unfit for human use. There are two distressing aspects to this situation: The first arises from the awareness that even with our pollution-producing economy, the growth within the United

States continues to require a doubling of the supply of electric energy and other energy forms about every twenty to thirty years. Industrial growth, "higher" standards of living, and leisure demand this rapid rate of increase as though the mark of an "advanced" society were synonymous with an *energy-consuming* society. The second difficulty arises from the fact that to reduce the pollution, even more energy must be consumed to filter or chemically treat the wastes. That is, the "system" has within it recycle features (later we shall call this *positive feedback*) that tend to accentuate rather than to reduce the energy problem.

Clearly the situation requires analysis to determine what rate and form of energy and material consumption per individual will permit a balance that can be maintained by future generations. The cybernetic approach lends itself to determination of such balance conditions, as we shall see. At this point we shall dwell a little longer on the historical aspects of automation principles that are relevant to our interest.

The role of automation

As the Industrial Revolution concentrated people in cities, what might have been a blessing turned out to be a curse as factories became prisonlike sweatshops for young and old. The idea that society bore responsibility for public welfare was not permitted to interfere with the profit motive of the new era. Fortunately the tide turned in the early 1900s, when laws were enacted to protect very young workers and the growth of labor unions improved both working conditions and wage scales. The higher wages added pressure to make industrial operations more mechanized and less dependent on the human operator. In many production plants, carrier systems transported material from machine to machine, beginning with raw material and ending with finished, packaged products at the other end of long production lines. While the early Industrial Revolution depended on machine design and ingenuity, the automation process required a good deal of scientific knowledge as well. The art of automatic-control and automatic-machine design made rapid progress.

The coming of *automation* is sometimes referred to as the *second phase* of the Industrial Revolution. One result of the developments was that production operations became so large and expensive in plant costs as to require public sharing in ownership of the plants by millions of stockholders. There evolved a remarkable form of push-pull between industrial managers and labor unions: labor unions pressing for higher hourly rates, fringe benefits, and fewer work hours per week; management pressing for higher profits, and shareholders watching for gains and losses in stock values.

During this period of automation, educational patterns also changed to make the scientific establishment more and more responsible for technological advances. Social adjustments were slower in coming. Before too long, overproduction became a serious problem in nations that had adopted an automated way of life and had not yet learned how to distribute the goods to people who needed them. Nor did overproduction eliminate poverty. Indeed the sense of poverty became extended, for as a result of the rapid industrial expansion that technology made possible, the poverty status became extended to whole nations that failed to take advantage of the new technology. The world is now made up of "have" nations against a large background of "have not" societies. The distinctions take on severer implications in that the poorer societies often are also faced with overpopulation and threats of mass starvation, while the "have" nations move toward greater technological advances.

As we shall see, the progress of societies can be analyzed in terms of cybernetic control principles involving either *positive* or *negative feedback*. Negative feedback tends to oppose large surges or departures of a variable from a normal or average condition, whereas positive feedback tends to accentuate changes in variables to send them either continuously upward or continuously downward. A progressive society is able to spare some of its energies and resources to put "money in the bank" in the form of agricultural and industrial research effort, exploration of minerals, improvement of soil, improvement of educational level, development and design of new production plants, and development of new products and new markets. This "money in the bank" draws "compound interest" that serves as *positive feedback* to increase the amounts of energy and resources that can be set aside for further improvements. In contrast, societies that must utilize all their effort and resources just to keep going, leaving nothing extra for improved education or development or research, suffer the stabilizing effects of *negative feedback*. In their case, "stability" means no increase in gross national product and no change from poverty, unfortunately. Conditions become worsened when the population spirals upward and thereby also causes the living standards to spiral downward, both having the nature of positive feedback. Thus while the rich get richer, the poor get poorer unless and until there is introduced the element of "money in the bank that draws interest" and produces growth that has some of the desirable features of positive feedback.

We shall see, however, that systems having positive feedback cannot go on forever. The *continued* presence of positive feedback sooner or later may cause a mechanical system to collapse. It is not any different in the case of societies that attempt to maintain positive feedback (continued increase) in relation to hourly rates for employees, profits for industries, the gross national product, use and misuse of natural resources, increased defense armament, or any other aspect of social life.

There is a next stage to all this, represented by the further exploitation of automation through use of computer technology, to which we now turn.

*The computer and automation**

The utilization of computers for more-sophisticated forms of automation is sometimes referred to as the *third phase* of the Industrial Revolution. The computer adds analytic and decision-making capabilities that take into account a great many variables, and do so very rapidly. Many mathematical concepts have been rendered "useful" for the first time because of the computer. These include game theory, partial differential equations, calculus of variations, linear algebra, linear programming, etc.

A virtue of the electronic computer is its ability to receive and to hold in memory many signals that represent *information,* given to it through the language of the binary code or of other symbols. The computer operates on this "information" through preselected techniques and in response to new signals or results of computations. In this respect it is like the body and sensory system of man, which

* There are many discussions available on computers and their uses. The reader will find the September 1966 issue of *Scientific American* to be interesting for an over-all view of the impact of computers on society and on technology, in addition to the other listed references.

receives signals from sensory receptors and transforms these into meaningful information.

The computer has advantages over the human system for computations that are complex and that require many approximations to complete. For example, computers are very useful for developing chemical processes that involve two or more solvents, wherein reaction rates vary with temperature and pressure and require whole families of stored data and calculations. Once the information is developed, another computer can take over the task of *controlling* the operation of the plant to maintain proper temperatures and pressures in the reaction vessels, check product quality, and make necessary adjustments in input or heat energy to maintain the quality.

Computer-type functions can also be incorporated in machines that fabricate parts that have unusual shapes, such as the large aluminum wings of airplanes. Here the controls are programmed in the form of equations, numbers, mechanical shapes, or in graph form. When combined with the use of telephone circuits, medical diagnoses or the contents of books or other information can be distributed over wide geographic areas with minimum delay. An example is frequently found in small units located at the counters of airline sales offices, from which within seconds that clerk can determine whether space is available on a flight in a distant part of the country. It was in 1953 that this writer was involved in establishing the first large electronic computer at a major university. At this writing there are over sixty thousand computers in use in the nation's business and research establishments. The use of computers for research and for teaching has increased to the point that few large universities are without them. The United States' investment in computers and associated equipment during 1971 was about $9 billion, with roughly another $14 billion to operate them. In the future, computers may be used in linguistics, in psychological analyses, and in language translation.

The picture is not altogether bright, however, for the dependence on computers and on automation brings risks as well. Computers require highly skilled human judgment for their use or misuse, but they are not "intelligent." They can compound human errors as well as reduce them. The shift to automation demands a higher educational level on the part of the designer, the builder, the assembler, the user, and in fact the general public. We are reminded of the prophecy of Alfred North Whitehead, who foresaw a half century ago both the advantages and threats that science offers:

"In the conditions of modern life the rule is absolute: the race which does not value trained intelligence is doomed."

A greater threat exists in connection with extensive use of computers for national defense. Military applications were among the first to promote the development of large computers. Computer systems serve as detectors of nuclear attack by an enemy, on the basis of which a decision could be made to launch an unimaginably devastating nuclear counterattack. There is always the risk that electronic systems may falter or fail or that misinterpretation of data may bring all-out nuclear retaliation where none is warranted. To the errors of judgment to which human beings are subject we thus add errors of electronic systems.

These, then, constitute the technological and social environments created by the three phases of the Industrial Revolution, within which we must discuss the concepts of cybernetics. We shall back off somewhat in time to review the recent history of that science.

The recent roots of cybernetics

The petroleum refineries of the United States were the first major industry to develop, in the late 1930s, central instrument and control systems for maintaining acceptable temperature and pressure conditions in the cracking towers. The more-sophisticated control principles appeared when the military agencies sought to develop improved systems for controlling gunfire, especially as airplanes became important during World War II. These controls made use of the servomechanism principle, involving pairs of motors that are so interconnected that when a small servomotor located at some convenient control position is rotated, another motor at another station rotates the same amount. The second motor could operate machines that direct a large cannon, for example. Servomechanism technology became exceedingly important as the speed of fighting aircraft became significant in relation to the speed of the missile. Antiaircraft fire required that corrections be made very quickly and that the controls anticipate where the target plane was likely to be on arrival of the missile. To make the corrections, the equipment had to incorporate computer functions as well as sophisticated control techniques.

Only slow mechanical computers were available at the beginning of World War II. To speed them up required wholly new developments revolving around electronic tubes and circuitry, with much larger memory capabilities for handling more variables. All these came into being in later years with the development of digital electronic computers, while during the war years there could only be identification of the new directions that had to be pursued, by someone such as Norbert Wiener of the Massachusetts Institute of Technology.

It was also Wiener's fertile mind that after the war brought together individuals who sought new interdisciplinary interests directed to purposes that are more humane than is the control of cannon fire.* In this connection the concept of *feedback* loomed important as a very general element even in the behavior of human systems. For if one is intent on following a moving object such as a bug with a pointer, it is not enough simply to move the arm in the direction of the bug. If the movements of the arm and hand are to be smooth and effective, each move must be accompanied by awareness of where the arm has moved and how much more it must go to reach the target. Such awareness comes only when there is *information feedback* from each move all the way to the target. Smooth action also requires speed control to avoid overshooting the mark. The idea of feedback was not new in mechanical or servomechanism systems, but it was relatively new in the context of the neurological system. Wiener and Julian Bigelow, working with Arturo Rosenblueth, who was then at Harvard Medical School, were able to confirm that there are indeed proprioceptive sensations that provide feedback information to the brain and that damage to these neural mechanisms reduces the simple act of picking up a pencil to uncontrolled oscillations of the arm.

The neurological interests brought the neurophysiologist Warren McCulloch and his mathematical associate W. Pitts strongly into the picture. McCulloch had interest in developing, for individuals who had lost the sense of sight or other senses, or limbs, improved

* See Professor Wiener's own accounting of these in his book on *Cybernetics*, in References.

means to make up for the loss. For example, in the case of the lost leg, while the artificial limb provides physical support and some means for locomotion, there are lacking feedback features which would give the wearer surer footing through knowledge of the progress of the limbs.

These, then, constitute the background of the 1940s and a few of the individuals who came together to explore phenomena that at the time had little relationship with each other. By the end of 1947 there was sufficient agreement among them to adopt the name *cybernetics* for *the science of control and communication in the animal and the machine.*

Inclusion of *communication,* and especially of feedback in the form of *information,* provided broad scope for this new science of cybernetics. It could thereby encompass all the capabilities of the large central computers that had not yet come into being. Those early thinkers had already begun to relate the new science to the brain, for the human brain is capable of receiving sensory signals and of processing these to become information that either immediately influences action or is stored for future use. In the case of the neural system, whatever information emerges as a product of neural processes becomes incorporated as awareness or memory, which may later become input. It is not different with the computer, which after completing its calculations may incorporate the answers in its own memory system for use with future calculations.

The similarities led to new boldness. Could a computing machine be designed to incorporate within itself the ability to alter its own characteristics? As we shall see, A. M. Turing of England proposed a *Turing machine,* which with the benefit of a code on a tape, can be guided by that code to become the universal automaton.

There were other interests that were even more daring: To what extent could computer/machine functions generate new information and thereby contribute some understanding of the nature of epistemology, or the basis, methods, and limitations of knowledge? What relevance could this have to the study of psychology or the behavior of individuals, if indeed the parallels between the brain and computers can be carried that far? To what extent could these same machinelike capabilities be extended to explain the reproductive processes of the cells of the body and the evolutionary processes in nature? Or to explain the origin of life?

Suffice it to say that most of these questions continue to be only questions to this day. It is fortunate, however, that within the broad and flexible framework of the concepts of cybernetics there are available new approaches wherewith to explore such avenues. Next we will introduce the concept of systems, in the context of a natural and social world that encompasses a remarkable combination of stability and instability, human and inhuman situations.

CHAPTER 2

The Makings of a "System"

To the thoughtful observer there are few "miracles"
more deserving of the term than are the commonplace
features of daily experience.

Equilibrium states in nature

There is a certain newspaper that boldly declares a policy of
presenting "All the News That's Fit to Print." On seeing the huge
size of its Sunday editions one might easily fear that during the
previous week the world must certainly have turned inside out. On
examining the contents, however, one soon realizes that the world
did not pursue more than its normal motion of one rotation in each
twenty-four hours. To be sure the paper contains items about
murders, disease, explosions, and perhaps a revolution or two in
far-off regions. On the whole, however, the critical reader is likely
to find himself turning pages rather hurriedly through advertisements,
the ups and downs of the stock market, and repetitious views by
columnists and editors. The impression the reader gains is more
likely to be of *sameness* than of exciting new happenings.
This in itself is quite remarkable, in view of all the interactions
that take place in a world of competing societies and threatening
elements. Within this geologic and biospheric complex, over three
billion humans and many, many billions of lesser creatures live
and breathe and compete for the necessities of life. Each organism
struggles to survive the fickle element of nature and death at the
hands of its neighbors. Within its own structure each plant, insect,
and animal lives and grows only because myriads of molecules
undergo devious co-operative movements and interactions to give
the organism substance, structure, and life. As if these hazards

were not enough, each organism is subject to the whims that
govern its own society. On occasion, the various societies become
antagonistic toward each other on an overwhelming, massive scale.

It is especially significant, therefore, that despite this total instability or dynamism in the physical and living world, this newspaper must rely, in order to fill its pages, on items that are routine,
expected, and rarely earth-shaking. The paucity of news need not
reflect failure on the part of this newspaper, however. Rather, it is
a forceful demonstration of the fact that, within the physical world
and the world of living things, influences are present that tend
to "stabilize" conditions. The "stability" is far from being a static
or a happy condition, however. Rather, the "equilibrium" represents
a tenuous balance between cyclic ups and downs, life and death,
and numbers of births versus numbers of deaths.

The stabilizing and cyclic features are easily observed within
our own bodies as we periodically take food and sleep to make up
for the depletion in the body. From the moment we awaken to
the time we finally relax in sleep, each of us utilizes sensory
means and locomotion to keep body and soul together, to avoid
walking in front of autos, to select foods that are likely to be good
for us, to take on jobs and tasks that provide money for food and
shelter, to prepare to make the morrow not too different from what
today might have been.

But while the process of survival is wondrously effective, we
know full well that it is not completely so. Survival itself would
prove destructive should each species multiply and overrun the
earth. As it is, each species becomes prey and sustenance for other
organisms in an almost endless chain, the greatest predator being
man and his society. In any case, there is retained some form of
equilibrium in the number ratio of each species to other species.
We should note, moreover, that true equilibrium is a mathematical
abstraction. In real life it usually exists only as a rough approximation.

Obviously there would be no news value in reporting that mankind had survived the week before by virtue of having killed and
used as food a million head of steer or a million tons of fish.
These represent the *normal* condition. The newsworthy item would
appear if men had failed to kill and consume and had thereby
dramatically changed the status quo in some respect or other.

Thus conditions do not change so dramatically or so often, and a good part of our interest in this volume has to do with determining the factors that make for this relative stability. For that, we must first determine what we mean by *systems,* and especially by the term *control systems.* That done, we shall return to qualify the ideas just presented by asking to what extent our equilibrium state, or "normal" state, remains unchanged. We shall find that while conditions do not change rapidly, neither do they remain unchanged for very long.

What is a system?

The dictionary suggests that a system may be a group of interacting items that form a unified whole or that are under the influence of forces in some relationship. It may refer to a group of stones on the beach, to an assembly of stars, or to a systematic assembly of words or symbols that may or may not have a functional relationship with each other. The word is used rather freely in the contexts of economic systems, social systems, political systems, mechanical systems, etc.

A good example of a system is a family of parents and children, which for our purposes offers many advantages over an assembly of stones on the beach. To the census taker, a "normal" family comprises parents and a certain number of children subdivided as boys or girls, the numbers changing slowly. The picture is radically more complex and interesting to anyone who is close enough to the family to observe the dynamic interactions and changes that take place hour after hour, moment after moment. The "normal" situation may turn out to be highly tenuous when, for example, a parent asks a child to do something or to cease doing something. This brings influence to bear on the child. The influence is rarely unidirectional, however, for the reaction of the child in turn reacts on the parent and indeed on the "system" as a whole. We may call reactions *feedback* in this system. The feedback can take various forms and produce varying results. For example, should the child choose to disobey the parent, the feedback could produce vastly different results as compared with the results that obtain when the child obeys.

The family example shares a number of features that characterize systems of most kinds. For example, note that introducing the idea of obedience versus disobedience introduces the element of *control*. Most systems that have significance to our world are likely to have controls and to be "designed" to use feedback influences through which to exercise control. To serve as a *control system*, in turn, implies the existence of a plan, or *design;* or a *purpose,* or objective. That is, the system is designed to do something, say to hold the rotational speed of a mechanical governor of a machine to a set value, to hold the temperature of a room at 72° F., or to require that a child conform to the rules and ethics of the household. We shall delve into these aspects presently.

Structure and function in systems

There are varieties of "structural" and functional relationships among the members of the family and with the physical and biological home environment: There are the biological relationships between husband and wife, between parents and children, and among the children. There is the role of the father as provider and protector and the functions of the mother as homemaker. There is a dwelling for shelter, cooking, sleeping, and family enjoyment. Note that many of the functions exist by virtue of *structural design* considerations. For example, the functions exercised by the father/provider and the functions performed by the mother are related to their own biological body structures. Note also that the relationships with the children change from the time of their infancy to the time when they leave for college. That is, changes in organizational or structural relationships will be accompanied by changes in functional relationships, in this case the result of the children's growing up.

In other words, a machine that is expected to perform a particular function must possess a structure that makes the function possible. In the case of biological systems the reverse may also be true, namely that the exercising of a function can change the structure. A common example is that of a child learning to play a musical instrument such as the piano: the faltering notes improve with practice to produce stronger fingers and better co-ordination with the brain.

Subsystems and levels of organization

A more careful examination of relationships within a family system reveals that each child has his own special body conditions, habits, biological processes, hopes, and fears, which are substantially different from those of the other children. The same is true of the parents, who despite the declaration that the two become one at marriage, remain two individuals who now share some common interests as well. In other words, we can regard each member of the family as a *subsystem* of the family system. On occasions when a subsystem member has a stomach ache or a broken leg, there comes the realization that he also has within himself parts and organs that enjoy some identity within the whole organism. That is, there are still-smaller subsystems within subsystems. The structure and function of the big toe of the right foot have a subsystem relationship to the larger subsystem of the foot and leg.

Nor does the chain of subsystems stop there, for the entire family with which we began is itself only a small subsystem of the community system. The chain goes on to larger and larger subsystems—the city, the state, the nation as a whole, the world. Nor does it stop with the world as a whole, as we shall see.

Open systems

We shall presently examine a typical system for controlling room temperature and shall note that it is an open system in the sense that to maintain its function the thermostat, motors, and boilers must be energized by electric power or by other sources of energy that are external to the system itself. That is, the system cannot function when isolated from outside influences, since it is not a self-sufficient, *closed system*. Living organisms are also open systems in that they also must derive nutrients and energy from the environment in order to function or to survive. However, there is required a very large leap from the electromechanical-chemical system noted above to reach the organizational and functional level of even the smallest of living cells of plants or animals. For one thing, living systems encompass many more variables than are found in non-living systems. More important, there is contained within even the smallest of living cells a greater degree of self-direction than exists in any physicochemical, non-living system. There exist in the cell biochemical processes whereby the cell can adapt to its own environment and in the process convert the nutrients and energy of the environment into more living organisms of its own kind.

Living cells join to form tissues and organs, and the latter make possible whole organisms of many kinds. That is, we are presented with levels that are vastly different from one another.* Even in simple plants there are specialized cells that serve in roots, leaves, or seeds, which perpetuate the species of the plant. The next higher level is sometimes called the *animal level,* at which sensory organs and motility of the organism become important. The *human level* might come next, with new capabilities in the form of speech, sense of time, and capability for symbolic reasoning. Human beings form *societies,* which introduce sufficient new variables to warrant putting them on a higher level. And some recognize the need to make room for a still higher level of "absolutes" and "inescapable unknowables," in the words of Boulding.

Open versus closed systems

At what point does an assembly become sufficiently large and inclusive to be called a total system and not simply a subsystem? The question may sound like a play on words and a matter of definition, which it is to some degree. There are nevertheless certain guidelines that are relevant for answering this question. In the case of the toe subsystem there are certain movements that one may study and attribute to the muscles and bones of the toe alone. The study would very quickly reveal the exchange of *energy* and of *information* between the toe and the rest of the body, without which there could be no toe function as we know it. We would therefore call the toe an *open system,* by which we mean:

(a) there is interchange of energy and of "information" between the subsystem and its environment,

(b) the interchange is such as to maintain some form of continuing equilibrium condition, and

(c) the relationship with the environment is such as to admit changes and adaptations, such as growth in the case of biological organisms.

The same reasoning explains why we would also call each member of our family an open system (or open subsystem) and make the community, the nation, and indeed the world as a whole all open

* See, for example, the chapter by Kenneth E. Boulding in the volume edited by Buckley, in References.

systems. The earth receives vast quantities of radiant energy from the sun, and we know well that without the in-pouring of that energy the biosphere as we know it would not exist.

What, then, is a *closed system?* Taking the converse of the three qualifications noted above, we suppose that a closed system is one that does not exchange energy or information with any body outside itself, although it may experience all kinds of internal changes. That is, the system is completely isolated. Can we, then, say that the universe as a whole represents a closed system? Possibly that is the situation, but the measurements that we are capable of making reveal only larger and larger spheres for the universe, and statements about the "exterior" of the universe seem to be entirely meaningless. On this basis there is no such thing as a truly closed or isolated, system.

While on the basis of these qualifications we cannot point to any "closed" system, the term is sometimes applied to very limited systems that perform their functions in a fixed manner without variation, such as a mechanical governor system that simply acts to maintain the rotational speed of a wheel to a set value. Sometimes the term is applied to systems in which the energy that is exchanged with the environment can be identified and measured. In this volume we shall generally regard systems as being "open," however.

Another explanation of open systems might be the paraphrased "No man is an island complete of himself." But if this is so, the reader may well ask how it is possible to study any subsystem completely, when interrelationships extend to the outer reaches of the universe. The answer is that while it is not possible to take into account *every* influence or interrelationship that bears on a particular situation or subsystem, we can often identify the significant factors that bear on a situation and limit the study to those factors. For example, the mother or father of our family can readily size up a situation involving a bruised knee and treat the bruise with salve without invoking arguments in favor of a national health program. Similarly a locksmith can be called on to repair the lock on the vault of a bank without involving arguments either on the merits of the nation's monetary system or even on the effectiveness of the bank president.

Aside from such trivial examples, however, it must be said that it is usually difficult to determine with confidence all the forces and factors that bear on a situation (or system)—which factors to take into account and which to neglect without serious prejudice to the results of the study. One of the great benefits that derive from electronic computers is the capability they offer for making quick order-of-magnitude approximations, followed by a succession of calculations that become better and better approximations toward final answers.

Interrelationships within systems

The interactions that occur among the members (or parts) of our chosen family system deserve a little more exploration, beginning with the sounding of the alarm clock that awakens the parents. The family's activities are thus initiated by a strictly mechanical gadget the virtue of which is to emit a loud sound or to turn on the more sophisticated clock radio. In either case, electrical or mechanical energy is translated into sound, which is also a form of mechanical energy. Of course the motion of molecules does not become sound until the ears of a listener respond to that motion and interpret the sensations to be sound. From there on, quite a few different transformations may take place as the hearers spring (or are dragged?) into action. Breakfast involves mental activity, muscle activity, heat energy, motion of pots and pans, oral requests and commands, and even promises and threats. From these observations we can identify three additional characteristics of systems:

1. It would be exceedingly difficult to isolate the strictly mechanical aspects of the system function from muscular and neural activities or from the interpretive processes of the brain. That is, there are very rapid and easy conversions of energy from one form to another form. (The mathematician would call these *transform functions*.) Note especially that, throughout the event, the *exchange of information* is a very vital part of the entire experience.

2. The interchange is not limited to the family system. Even as the day begins, there is involvement with the outer world. Breakfast may face a crisis if the power lines fail to keep the electric clock running or if the milk delivery should fail. The members of the family may fail to get to their schools or to their jobs if the transportation system should fail. Obviously this subsystem has

continuous exchange of energy and of information with the larger system of which it is a part.

3. There develop from this continuous interchange *time-sequential relationships* as well. We are accustomed to thinking that every effect has a cause. For instance, should the eggs burn we would readily assume that the heating was excessive. The eggs are cooked sunny side up because that is the way father likes them; or at least that is the ready answer. Actually every event evolves from a chain of events. We might find, for example, that there were many arguments and many feedback repercussions before the eggs were fried sunny side up or before Junior appeared properly dressed and combed for breakfast.

We are now ready to return to the question of the stability of situations and of systems.

The evolution of equilibrium states

The small child of our family may suddenly decide to resist parental authority and may have to be helped to return to normality by means of restoring forces such as a slap on his bottom. Let us assume that parental authority is thereby restored. How complete is restoration? Has the system been returned exactly to the condition that obtained before the surge of resistance? The answer is that the system is not exactly as it was at the start and never will be again. The incident will have brought some new ideas and new attitudes and a different background from which to approach the next experience.

Similar changes occur in most other systems, especially when they involve living organisms. This spring may appear to be the same as earlier springs, but closer examination reveals that neither the rocks and earth, nor the rivers, nor the populations of living organisms will ever be exactly as they were before. An upward surge of the financial stock market may initiate a selling spree that returns prices to the former level, but the "restored" conditions are rarely (or never) identical with the initial condition with respect to distribution of prices, ownership of stock, or attitudes. There is always an "increment of difference."

Daily "increments of difference" can be identified as one carefully examines each edition of a newspaper. The increments accumulate and in time produce rather dramatic changes, such as are immediately apparent when one compares a 1900 issue of the New York *Times* with a current issue. The changes over that period of years in technology, industry, financial issues, community life, fashions, world political situation, and social attitudes have been considerable. Within the biological world the "increments" are often identifiable even from one generation to the next generation. For while genes of the cell see to it that each new cell is as nearly identical as possible to the original cell during cell division, the genetic processes that require the union of a male and a female element to produce progeny assure that *there will be some change but not major change* from one generation to another. For the progeny will surely differ from parents who are similar but not identical in their biological make-up.

Thus we see that there are two aspects to natural phenomena. On the one hand there are forces that resist severe, sudden changes, as when a downward surge in the stock market brings into play a greater demand to buy. The price of meat at the store suffers seasonal fluctuations, and many other aspects of nature and of man's social patterns show daily, monthly, or yearly alternations. On the other hand, the cycles are rarely or never exactly overlapping or identical. In fact, if one were to plot these variables on a graph it would be readily evident that the cycles "ride" long evolutionary trends. Stock-market quotations and the population characteristics of a city are likely to follow long-range trends upward or downward. The price of meat certainly rides a long upward trend.

In other words, there are within nature both forces that maintain equilibrium of sorts by resisting rapid changes, and forces that demand changes by slower, evolutionary processes. There is often a daily cycle, a yearly cycle, and a cycle that is measured in terms of a full lifetime, from birth to death. The passing of each year brings emergence of new hormonal and other processes that represent growth, approach to maturity, and finally of old age. There are contained within the seeds of the procreative processes remarkably effective means not only for reproducing nearly identical cells for the new organism, but also a fairly complete "program" for its continued biological growth until a form of maturity is achieved and the "ontogenic* purposes" of the organism are fulfilled within its own lifetime. The organism is a *self-organizing system* that converts the energy and nutrients and non-material influences of its environment to fulfill its natural "purposes." We must assume that this is made possible by the incorporation within the organism of *information* in forms that are suitable for direction of each day's activities and also the activities of its whole lifetime. Some writers refer to the organism as exhibiting "equifinality," as though it had a goal of its own from beginning to end.

What might be inferred from this with respect to the "phylogenic purposes" of a species? The "information" that guides the development of each organism throughout its lifetime is itself the product of evolutionary change and development. The question is tantalizing, as are so many other questions that pertain to living organisms.

* *Ontogeny* refers to the life history or development of an individual organism, as distinguished from *phylogeny*, or the evolution of a race or group.

CHAPTER 3

On the World in Motion

". . . irresistible developments hidden in extreme slowness—
extreme agitation concealed beneath
a veil of immobility—the entirely new insinuating itself
into the heart of the monotonous repetition of the
same thing."*

Pierre Teilhard de Chardin (1881–1955)

The cybernetic world is a world of actions and interactions, of forces and continuous energy exchanges and conversions. Indeed the most significant characteristics of both non-living and living things usually derive from the quality of their movements, and these in turn are determined by the forces to which they are subjected. For this reason a study of cybernetics requires some understanding of forces, energy, and motion. Solid ice differs from its liquid and vapor counterparts only by the reduced agitation of its molecular parts. Motions associated with the processes of life range from subtle molecular movements all the way to movements of large bodies. And as implied so beautifully in the quotation from Teilhard de Chardin, the "entirely new" may emerge with little ostentation and only as a slight change of movement from a background of utter sameness. We shall return to this "entirely new" in Chapter 10, when probing the origin of life. At this time we shall explore a few features that accompany things in motion, for which purpose it will be useful to utilize the approach with which motion of objects was first clearly explained, in the period of Isaac Newton.

* *The Phenomenon of Man* (New York: Harper & Row, 1961). Reproduced by permission of Harper & Row.

The unchanging world

If we were asked to identify unchanging aspects of nature, a ready answer might point to the solid earth or to the "fixed" starry canopy above. A slightly more sophisticated answer might add the unending movements of the sea, and the repeated cycles of day and night and of the planets. That is, both that which does not move and that which moves in a fixed pattern may have the quality of being "unchanging." It was Isaac Newton (1642–1727) who first saw through these differences and explained the matter simply and clearly in his first law of motion:

> Every body persists in its state of rest, or of uniform motion in a straight line, unless it is compelled to change from that state by forces impressed upon it.

The ancients who built many wonderful structures and traced the paths of the planets in detail failed to uncover this simple fact. The reasons for the failure lay at least in part in the difficulty of finding situations in everyday life in which bodies in motion are permitted to move altogether without interference. Even a smooth ball rolling on a long track eventually comes to a stop as a result of frictional losses. And the statement that things at rest remain at rest probably appeared to be too trivial to even mention, for everyone knows that tables and chairs do not start moving about on their own. Fortunately Newton saw the deeper significance of a body persisting at rest. Note, however, that even in the case of heavenly bodies the motion is in orbits around the sun (or around the earth in the case of the moon) rather than in a straight line. This makes Newton's intuition all the more remarkable, and the example makes us wonder whether we in our age also fail to identify some rather basic "laws" of living processes and behavioral situations for the reason that they appear trite or too commonplace.

The Newtonian principle that objects remain at rest except as they are subjected to external forces holds in other situations as well. The "objects" may just as properly be an individual's mood of the moment, or the trend of international events; and the "external forces" may be the turn of a valve, a spoken word, or the national build-up of military "defense."

This changing world

The world at rest or in uniform motion was only a beginning for Newton. His next concern was the processes by which things change—that is, by which objects at rest are moved or moving objects are brought to a halt. We can imagine how he might have reasoned through this problem: The heavier an object the harder one must push to get it moving. There are therefore differences in resistance to motion among objects due to some property that we call the *mass* of the object. The larger the mass the harder one must push to start it moving.

One soon discovers that the push required to move an object also varies with the *acceleration,* or the rate at which one tries to move the object: the faster the object is to go (or the larger the social or educational change one tries to initiate) the larger must be the force to get it moving. A series of measurements soon reveals Newton's second law, which in its simplest form says that an object of mass M will move with an acceleration a that is proportional to the magnitude of the force F applied to move the object. (Thinking in more-general and less-precise terms, we can imagine that the relationship may not be too dissimilar between the volume of sales of a product and intensity of the advertising campaign to sell the product.) This second law in fact offers a good way to measure the inertial properties, or *mass,* of objects, since our awareness of muscular force is more direct than is our awareness of the mass of an object. In the mechanical world it has been more useful to develop a standard of mass, which is embodied in the *standard kilogram,* kept in the form of a cylinder of platinum at the Bureau Internationale des Poids et Mesures, at Sèvres, near Paris. With this standard for the mass, the meter as the measure of length, and the second as the measure of time, the unit called the *newton* is defined as that force which, when applied to the standard kilogram accelerates it at a rate of one meter per second during each second that the force is applied. When a one-kilogram mass is suspended from a calibrated scale (Fig. 1), the scale indicates the pull of gravity to be 9.8 newtons. Thus we see that the pull of gravity, and therefore the acceleration it gives to falling objects, corresponds to 9.8 newtons.

If the object being pushed or pulled is not free to move away, it

34 THIS CYBERNETIC WORLD

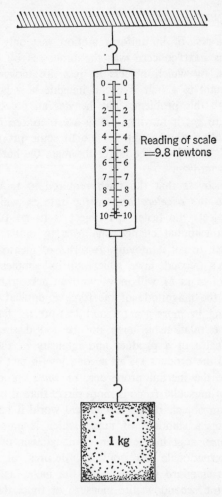

Fig. 1. Pull of gravity on 1-kg mass extends the spring of the balance to indicate 9.8 N.

may instead stretch, like the spring scale of Fig 1. There is a linear relationship between the pull on a spring and the way it increases in length. That is, the amount that a spring stretches is proportional to the intensity of the pulling force and the stiffness coefficient of the particular spring being stretched. This linear relationship between the stretch of a spring and the pull, known also as Hooke's law, also expresses the magnitude of the *restoring force* that a spring exerts to return to its normal length. We shall find that the same phenomenon exists in other situations as well, where the more a variable is displaced, the stronger are the restoring forces that are generated by the displacement. This is true whether one is dealing with human tempers, with a violin string, prices of commodities, or extremes in political action, although in these cases the relationship is not likely to be as linear as is the case with a spring. That is, while human patience is tried in some proportion to the magnitude of the cause of irritation, it would be difficult to identify a constant factor for the proportionality.

Work and energy

Everything we do in the course of a day involves *force* and *energy*. This is true whether we sit or stand, lift a weight, or push a ball or a shopping cart in the supermarket. Each activity requires push or pull on the part of the muscles of the body. There can be considerable differences in the *magnitude* and *form* of the push or pull, however. It takes very little force to roll a ball along the floor compared to the force required to push a baby carriage. We say it is "real work," or that it takes more energy to push an automobile. We also become aware that the energy expended (as revealed by the tiredness of our muscles) increases with the distance that we push an object. That is, the work done is proportional to the distance. In fact the tiredness of muscles, energy expended, and *work done* are all equal to *force times distance*. This relationship defines work done in moving an object.

Where does this energy go? In the case of the rolling ball, most of it becomes *kinetic energy,* or energy related to the velocity of the body, while a little of it is lost in friction with the ground. The same is true of the motion of the baby carriage or automobile, except in these cases the greater frictional forces (or drag) will stop the vehicle more quickly than is the case with the rolling ball. We can say that when we push these objects *along a level ground,* the work we do goes into *kinetic energy* and into *frictional losses*. The kinetic energy is equal to one half the product of the mass and the square of the velocity, and when left alone this energy becomes dissipated in frictional losses.

The above discussion assumed the ground to be level. What if the ball or the carriage were to be pushed up a slight grade? The first difference would be in the greater force required to push objects uphill. The reason is that in addition to the kinetic energy that the object acquires from the work done, there is present also a building up of *potential energy,* which is related to the mass and the *change in height.* Therefore the work we do in pushing such objects may go into kinetic energy, potential energy, or friction, or be divided among all three.

A good example of energy conversion is the roller coaster in the amusement park. The cars of the coaster are first pulled by electric motors up to the highest point of the track system. When the cars reach the top, they have only potential energy. When the cars start rolling down, this potential energy is rapidly converted to kinetic energy. But because the tracks go up again, the energy is once more transformed into potential energy at the peaks. The rider will notice, however, that each succeeding "peak" is built lower than the last one, to take into account the energy lost in friction in going from peak to peak. In fact by the end of the ride most of the energy will have been dissipated in frictional losses, thereby slowing down the cars and contributing to the relief of the rider.

In the case of pulling on a coil spring, the work done goes largely into potential energy. However, when a mass attached to the spring is suddenly released, the stretching and release of the spring send the system into oscillation as the potential energy is transformed into kinetic energy, and vice versa.

One of the major principles of nature seems to be that, *in a closed system, energy is conserved.* This is readily seen in the simple oscillating spring system. In a second example, the work done in pulling the roller coaster to its first peak can be accounted for exactly at any later instant of time, for the same total energy is present either as kinetic energy, potential energy, or as heat loss in friction. In other systems some of the energy may also be in electrical, magnetic, or chemical form. That is, energy may be changed from one form to another, but never lost. The mass of an object is not so conserved, however. As we have found during our own century, the atoms that make up matter can be converted from one form to another, and some of the mass made to "disappear" and to show up as energy. In fact the destructiveness of atomic bombs derives from sudden conversion of a few pounds of uranium or plutonium atoms into energy.

The action-reaction principle

Newton's third law says:

To every action there is an equal reaction; or the mutual actions of two bodies upon each other are always equal, and in opposite directions.

Ordinarily we substitute the term *force* for *action* and *reaction*, and say that a force F_1 applied to an object gives rise to a force F_2 that is exactly equal to F_1 but has opposite direction and acts on the other body. Whatever pulls or pushes an object, is pulled or pushed by that object with an equivalent force. When you press a stone with your finger, the finger is also pressed by the stone. When a book or other object is held on the palm of the hand, it presses down because of the pull of gravity, and the hand must exert an exactly equal upward force to keep in a fixed position.

These are the laws of Newton to which we made reference in Chapter 1 as being the basis for the rationalism and age of reason that followed his period. Every "effect" had a "cause," and the cause-and-effect relationship could be made very precise. The preciseness of these laws and their success in dealing with mechanical situations was such as to dominate thinking processes for many generations to come. They constitute fundamental features of cybernetic systems as well, but with two important modifications: For the first, cybernetic concepts and interests are not limited to mechanical or electromechanical systems for the sake of preciseness; the real phenomena and experiences of nature or of human beings are not so limited. The second difference has to do with the "longer view" that one must give to phenomena and to situations, for whereas the Newtonian laws concern themselves only with the speed and energy that are given to a stone when one applies force to hurl it, the cyberneticist may concern himself with all the events that led to the throwing of the stone and with the direct and indirect repercussions that follow and are intertwined with the event. Preciseness usually suffers in the analysis, but the experience is more likely to ring true in all its complications.

Extension to statistical situations

Thus far our examples of Newton's laws have involved single forces acting on single bodies. While such applications are important, they constitute only a fraction of the situations involving forces and acceleration of masses. What happens, for example, when we walk, and feel pushed, in a strong wind? Although the forces are invisible, the experience is just as real as if we were being pushed by human hands. From other information, we know that the air molecules are in a state of agitation—colliding, and passing their energy and momentum back and forth among each other. When a large obstacle such as our own body stands in their way, the bouncing of each molecule exerts a tiny force on the body, just as the ball bouncing against a wall transfers momentum to the wall. There are vast numbers of collisions with molecules from all sides, but the direction from which the wind blows having a higher concentration of molecules (number of molecules per cubic centimeter), the extra collisions develop a net force in the "downstream" direction that becomes *flow of energy*. A difference in concentration is likely to produce flow of materials and energy in a direction toward lower concentrations. When, however, an obstruction (such as our body) is in the path of the flow of energy or flow of particles, the body feels the very force that we experience in the wind.

We see that in this and in many other situations the net results of the push-pull are obtained as a statistically determined quantity involving vast numbers of molecules. Do the laws of motion as given by Newton apply to the statistical net results? They do. Do they also apply to the individual molecules that collide in so many different ways and in such numbers? We have no reason to say that they do not. On the other hand, we can no longer say with assurance that at the atomic level there exists a firm cause-and-effect relationship such as exists for large objects. Our means are not adequate for testing such things, and determinism as prescribed by Newton's laws may have to make room for some kind of indeterminacy.*

* See Chapter 13, "Transition from Determinacy to Indeterminacy," in Part I of *Introduction to Natural Science*, Parsegian et al., in References.

Extension to social situations

The concepts presented for motion of a particle apply in the same way to many other variables in nature. In every metabolic process by which food is converted to energy in the body, there is a *rate* for the metabolic process. There is a rate for every chemical process, as well as a rate for the increase of the gross national product. The national income can go down as well as up, and a chemical reaction may act in the reverse direction as well.* To vary the rate of change there must be acceleration or deceleration similar to that observed in the motion of particles. The data for the metabolic processes, chemical reactions, or gross national product can be plotted as if they were displacement values. Average rates can be determined by taking the ratio of the amount of change to the time interval for that change.

In economics and when analyzing the movement of dollars or of goods, it is possible to identify quantities that seem to correspond to Newton's three laws. We can refer to the existence of a "reaction" to every action, or go further and talk of reaction in terms of *feedback* that may have circuitous routing. Thus while the non-mechanical situations are not likely to be as clearly analyzable as are mechanical systems, they share common features nevertheless.

Forces may develop from the interaction of vast numbers of molecules or of populations of insects or of human beings. Or the forces may be due to ideas, information, or misinformation; to hunger, love of freedom, or hate. Although in every complex situation the impact of individual interactions may pull every which way, a statistical summation often reveals the direction as well as the magnitude of the *net force* that bears on a particular situation. What happens then? An analogy with the second law says that the system will "give" under that force, but that the rate at which it gives way is dependent both on the magnitude of the force and on the property of the system corresponding to "mass." Just as the mass of a material object gives it the property of inertia, the property of resisting change, so each situation (be it population numbers, attitude toward religion,

---

* The belief existed even in early days with such men as Laplace and Poisson that the findings from celestial mechanics could be applied to "social mechanics."

or attitude of one nation toward another) contains within itself a property of "inertia" or "mass." In many social situations it is information, or rather misinformation, that develops pressures likely to produce the most rapid changes. An interesting feature is that within a population there is likely to be one magnitude of "inertia" (or responsiveness) to political issues, another to religious issues, and in fact quite varied responsiveness to each category of questions and issues that are a part of the life of a community.

The principle that there is a reaction to every action is likely to be useful in dealing with any situation. The main difference is that whereas in the mechanical situation a man on roller skates immediately goes backward in reaction to his pushing against a wall, the reaction in social situations may be long delayed and circuitous. We would sometimes have difficulty in identifying the reactions, which we now would call "feedback."

The nature of heat energy

Our extension of Newton's laws to the unseen world must be given special consideration in relation to heat energy and the laws of thermodynamics, the importance of which will be revealed especially in Chapter 10. It was no accident that a Prometheus was invoked by the ancients to steal fire from the resources of the heavens even at the risk of eternal torture, in order to bring it to earth for man's use. Absence of heat energy brings the stillness of death, while the warmth of fire brings life to the body as the sun gives life to the plant. Fire in the hearth was sacred to the Greeks and the Romans, and the object of near worship in religions such as Zoroastrianism. The Greeks saw fire as one of the four basic elements, the others being earth, water, and air. In the centuries that followed there came the "caloric," or "fluid," theory, which pictured heat as an actual substance that flowed into and out of objects. It was not until the late seventeenth century that the English philosopher John Locke (1632–1704) surmised that: ". . . heat is a very brisk agitation of the insensible parts of the object. . . . What in our sensation is heat, in the object is nothing but motion." Ultimately this truer concept established the *kinetic theory of heat* and the laws of thermodynamics.

Since Newton's laws apply to motion of particles, one might presume that this fortunate development would have become useful for the analysis of the motion of particles that are associated with heat energy. Such was not to be, however. For in contrast with the objects ("apples," moon, etc.) studied by Newton, the particles that experienced "brisk agitation" could not be seen, since they were of atomic dimensions. Moreover, as time revealed more details the *numbers* of the agitated particles were seen to be so enormous and their motion so uncertain that it became impossible to think of them in terms of individual movements. In the case of gases and liquids especially, the particles collide with each other in every conceivable way, so that at each instant of time there exist wide fluctuations in the velocities and directions of motion of the particles. For example eighteen grams of water (one mole) contains 6×10^{23} molecules* of water, and one cubic centimeter of air contains over 10^{19} molecules. Even at ordinary room temperatures, these molecules are in a state of extreme agitation, colliding and exchanging energy with each other. The possibility that these movements and collisions could be studied in terms of Newton's laws seemed to be forever eliminated.

Another door was opened, however, with realization that the very vastness of the numbers of colliding particles give the system a *statistically stable character.* That is, while in a container of gas it is impossible to know what any particular gas molecule is doing from one instant to the next, the fact that the system as a whole remains unchanging with time (at constant temperature) indicates that the *averages* of internal conditions do not change. In such an isolated system there develops a state of *statistical equilibrium.* We can therefore assume that the gas molecules of a container held at a fixed temperature (in a state of statistical equilibrium) will have velocities that are charactertistic of the gas at that temperature.

The laws of thermodynamics

Among the most important of the principles that describe physical processes are the laws of thermodynamics. These have to do with energy exchanges and with trends in the flow of energy, especially heat energy. All natural and man-made processes involve energy utilization or energy transformations, and for this reason the principles or laws of thermodynamics apply whether one is admiring the

---

* The number is therefore 6 followed by twenty-three 0's.

beauty of a rose, performing an experiment, driving an automobile, or analyzing cosmic processes. We shall note a few features of the laws in a simple setting, then explore their significance for the larger physical and the living world.

There is what is called the *"zeroth" law* of thermodynamics, which simply confirms the common observation that when two bodies that have the same temperature are placed against each other their temperatures *remain* the same. That is, there is no *net* flow of heat energy from one to the other. This does not mean that the molecules are at rest or that there is no heat exchange between them. It simply means that as much heat goes one way as the other way, without any *net* exchange between the bodies. The two bodies are in *statistical equilibrium* with each other. This leads directly to the *first law of thermodynamics,* which states that *in any closed system energy is conserved.* If heat is added to a system, it can be accounted for in the sum of increase in internal energy of the system plus work done by the system against its surroundings. For example, when heat is added to a block of ice to convert it to steam, the added heat is equal exactly to the increase in internal energy of the air and water molecules (steam) plus the work that the steam does in expanding.

Going now to two objects that are not at identical temperatures, the *second law of thermodynamics* says that there will be a *net flow* of heat energy, and always from the warmer to the colder body. A hot cup of coffee loses heat to the colder surroundings; the coffee will never *of itself* warm up to become hotter than its surroundings.

A better expression for the second law utilizes probability considerations. It is based on the observation that when certain states are "more probable" to the system than are other states, *the system will always move in the direction of the more probable states.* For example, it is not at all likely that a hot cup of coffee will remain hotter than its surroundings for very long; conversely it is very probable that the hot coffee will lose heat and assume a temperature that approaches the temperature of its surroundings. On this recognition the second law declares that "what is the more likely will occur," and the coffee will cool down.

There are other implications of this second law that are even more significant. Continuing with the same example, we note first that when the coffee is hot the molecules of water collide vigorously, as do the air molecules of the room, all in a generally chaotic manner. However, over and above the chaotic or random movements there is a *net flow* of energy from the coffee outward into the air. Whether hot or cold, the total energy content of the cup and of its room environment remains constant, in accordance with the first law. (That is, we can assume that none of the heat energy leaves the room.) When the coffee is cold, however, there is *no longer any net flow* of energy in any direction, although the molecules of coffee and of the air are still in very rapid motion and collision with one another. In fact their individual movements and kinetic energy are not much reduced from the energy they had when the coffee was hot. Now, however, we can say that the system, lacking any net flow of energy, is even more chaotic, *disordered,* random, undirected. Although there is still lots of energy in the system (since even a room temperature of 68° F. is 528° F. above absolute zero) the state of statistical equilibrium renders that energy useless and incapable of doing work. From the "ordered" state in which the hot coffee represents a "purposed," organized situation with heat energy concentrated in one part and flowing outward, the system is now reduced to a condition of equilibrium and greater molecular disorder (or reduced order).

The change from ordered to less-ordered states is a measurable, definite quantity to which the name *entropy* is applied. It is the factor that takes into account the fact that while the total energy content of a closed system remains constant, with increase of entropy less and less of that energy can be made useful. Entropy is defined as follows: When heat is added slowly to a system that is at temperature T (expressed in degrees Kelvin), there is an increase in the entropy of the system, (obtained by dividing the added heat by the absolute temperature). For example, when 18 grams (a mole) of ice melts to become water, there is an *increase* of entropy of 5.3 calories/degree.* There is also an accompanying *increase of disorder,* in that molecules in the fluid state have much less organization than those in the solid state, where they also vibrate vigorously but are held in fixed relationship to each other.

* The process requires 1447 calories to convert a mole (18 g) of ice to water. Melting ice has a temperature of 0° C or 273° Kelvin. Therefore this reaction gives an increase in the entropy of the system amounting to $1447/273 = 5.3$ cal./deg.

The second law and the concept of entropy are given still another interpretation, which relates entropy to the logarithm of the probability of states, namely that *the entropy is higher for states that have the higher probability of occurrence.*

Since the state with "cold coffee" (a state of statistical equilibrium) is the more probable state, entropy is higher for equilibrium states. Indeed for every process taking place in a system that is relatively "closed," without heat flow into or out of the system, the *entropy always increases.* The second law therefore states:

When a closed system containing a large number of particles
is left to itself, it assumes a state of maximum entropy;
that is, it becomes as disordered as possible.

The law leads to the conclusion that in such closed or isolated systems, although the *total* energy content of the system remains unchanged, the energy becomes less and less useful as the molecules of the system become more and more disordered. Every evidence that we can gather from measurements on earth and involving outer space seems to confirm this law and to spell the ultimate degeneracy of energy, and "death" of the universe. Of course we cannot know what other factors exist at present that are beyond our ken and the range of our measurements.

We titled this chapter "On the World in Motion," and described a few phenomena involving matter in motion such as might have been observed even when the earth first took shape five or more billion years ago. About two billion years ago there entered into the picture a new kind of "motion" in the form of living organisms. Or as stated beautifully by Teilhard de Chardin in the quotation that begins the chapter: ". . . the entirely new insinuating itself into the heart of the monotonous repetition of the same things." The laws affecting matter in motion did not change, nor did the laws of thermodynamics lose validity. However, the beginning of life on earth did introduce a subsystem of living things within which the second law of thermodynamics seemed to be momentarily by-passed. For while the over-all trend in the flow of energy continued toward equalization and a state of maximum disorder and maximum entropy, the direction was reversed within living organisms: Through the marvelous processes of photosynthesis and of metabolism, scattered atoms became collected and organized into organisms that could live and breathe and add vastly new kinds of "motions" and biochemical and mental processes to enrich the earth. Indeed our interest in the "motions" of this chapter will have significance only to the extent that they relate to the newer motions and functions that emerged two billion years ago.

We shall have occasion to return to the concept of entropy and will find especial interest in relating it to information and information theory.

CHAPTER 4

Functional Elements of Control Systems

> As no man is an island complete of himself, and no
> event emerges unrelated to other events, so every cause
> is itself an effect, and every effect a cause that presses
> both forward and as often backward to challenge
> its own origins.

From general descriptions it is time to turn to an examination of the functional details of control systems. The formalized concepts of cybernetics as we understand them today emerged from several decades of down-to-earth experience with control of industrial and other processes, and the earlier experiences still offer the most useful examples through which to introduce the basic concepts of cybernetics. On occasion one feels that even technical papers that are heard at professional-society meetings could offer more value if the authors would occasionally recall these basic concepts.

Why control systems

One of the accomplishments of the Newtonian period was to give a firm base to the concept that in physical situations at least, things do not happen without a causal force. A stone does not begin to move or come to a stop of its own volition. In this chapter we shall extend the concept in three directions:

(a) The first extension takes into account the fact that in most situations surrounding an event (such as hurling a stone), the immediate event is itself only one part of a larger picture that includes other parts or related events. For example, there is a *person* who throws the stone, and the throwing has relation to some *cause,* or *purpose*. We shall therefore view each event or situation as constituting a *system of interrelated parts or events*.

(b) The second extends the action-reaction principle to include a longer time span within the context of the larger system. In our example, when a stone is thrown there is often a *feedback* effect, as when the one at whom the stone is thrown hurls it back. Much of our interest therefore will have to do with exploring circuitous feedback influences (reactions) that result from an event, and determining how they reflect back on the cause of the event.

(c) Most situations, and therefore also the systems that we analyze, may include material things (stones) and human beings along with biological processes and the less tangible thought processes. This being the case, we shall disregard distinctions between the living and the non-living world wherever feasible.

Having determined (with Newton) that the processes and fluctuations of nature can go their own way without inviting human interference, we must quickly qualify this by saying that there are important cases in which it is necessary to interfere in order to modify the natural pattern or hold fluctuations to small changes. For example, the farmer may not want to depend entirely on natural rainfall to assure a good crop, so he intervenes by irrigating the fields against the time when there will not be enough rainfall. Because in the course of the year there are wide fluctuations in the temperature of the earth, he installs a control system in his home to keep the temperature within comfortable limits.

Indeed many types of controls are involved in our daily life. The human body has a remarkable control system to maintain its own temperature within very close limits. The body's motor functions, by which we move arms and legs in a predetermined manner, are made possible only because of the operation of superb integrating and control systems. Industrial production relies heavily on control of temperature, pressure, chemical composition. Applications are extensive in community and national life, and although systems and applications vary widely we shall find that they have common features as well.

We shall now identify some of the characteristics that are common to both mechanical and non-mechanical control systems, beginning with simple experiments that the reader can perform in his own home.

Walking "blind"

The essential features of a control system are revealed very nicely by the simple process of walking down a narrow aisle or corridor in one's own home. Normally the act is so automatic that the essential functions associated with such a walk are glossed over. But if the eyes are shut during the walk, simulating the walk of a blind person, the details are revealed very clearly.

When we start to walk down the corridor of our home like a blind person, the first point to note is that there is a *motive*, or *purpose*, in the act. Control systems are usually regarded as having a "purpose," and cybernetics is said to involve decisions and to be *goal-directed*. In the case of systems such as regulators on machines or temperature controls, the "purpose" is built in by design and construction. In contrast, systems such as the human body possess flexibility and ability to make decisions that are suited to new situations.

At any rate, a mental process brings into play muscle or *motor activity* and the *energy resources* of the body for execution of the walk. Since what we are trying to do is to walk through the corridor without running into the walls, the *variable* is our position in relation to the corridor walls. Our eyes being shut, we must introduce another *sensor*, or detector device, with which to know where we are in relation to the walls (that is, to know when the direction of our walk needs correction). This can be in the form of a cane in one hand, which we move back and forth in front of us as the blind do. Then as we proceed cautiously down the corridor, the cane tapping a wall on, say, the left side provides a signal in the form of noise to the ear and the feel of the cane in the hand. The brain interprets the signal as *feedback* to initiate a corrective move to the right, whereupon we proceed forward until the cane touching the right wall again signals the need for corrective action, this time to the left. We finally complete the walk, but only after a number of "hunting," cyclic moves from one side to the other.

Note that in this control system there are involved:

(a) a *variable*, which is our body position in relation to the center line or the walls of the corridor;

(b) a *sensor device* (in this case the cane, the hearing and touch senses, and the interpretive functions of the brain) that is sensitive and responsive to changes or departures of the variable;

(c) a *motor means* whereby corrective action can be taken, in this case provided by the neural and muscle system;

(d) *energy source* to provide the energy that is always required for any kind of activity, and finally

(e) *feedback,* whereby the state of the variable as communicated by the sensors becomes utilized to effect control action.

These five functions are involved in every control system, whether the control is of blood pressure, salt concentration in the cell, the temperature of a room, or the control of an industrial process. Unfortunately it is not often easy to identify a specific part of the system to correspond with each of the functions.

There are several additional observations we can make on this simple walk that again apply very generally. We have already noted that the walk is not likely to be straight but to have an oscillatory character, back and forth from wall to wall as though "hunting" for the mid-position. Note also that while we can negotiate the walk successfully while walking slowly, with faster walk there will come a speed above which we cannot respond to the signals quickly enough to avoid running into the walls. The elements of a successful control system must be sufficiently fast as well as sufficiently sensitive to satisfy the specific requirements for each control function.

Next note that the corrective steps that follow feedback must be *negative.* That is, the brain must initiate a corrective move that *opposes* the original move that carries us toward a wall. Since we ran into the left wall because our direction was too much to the left, the corrective increment must change our direction slightly to the right. If the "correction" were the reverse, it would only support the initial direction and become *positive feedback,* which would carry us more quickly against the wall.

Finally we note that the system involves a remarkable series of transformations, or *transform functions.* Brain activity initiates muscle activity of the legs and arms. The tapping of the cane produces sound and sensory signals to the hand and to the ears, becoming converted again by the brain into significant *information.* Body metabolism energizes the whole operation. The conversions take place even in electromechanical systems such as those controlling the temperature of a room, to which we turn next.

Control of temperature

Most heating systems provide control devices for maintaining the temperature of the rooms within certain limits during cold weather. These are usually simple systems of the "on-off" type (which we shall describe presently) that take their control information from a thermostat located in some part of the room. In this case the *variable* is the temperature of the air in the room. What is meant by *temperature?* Actually the sensations of temperature that the body feels do not give the story. The temperature of a room is high or low depending on whether the molecules that make up the air have relatively more or less kinetic energy, i.e., whether they are moving fast or slow. We cannot even see the molecules, much less measure their velocity; therefore we must look for *sensor devices* that change in some measurable or detectable way with changes in the temperature. Such a sensor device is the thermostat, in which a bimetal* strip bends more or less in response to changes in its own temperature that are brought about by collisions with molecules in the air. The more frequent and hard the collisions between the molecules and the bimetal strip, the more it warms up and bends.

But now we must design the sensor device to initiate motor action. In the case of the thermostat, the bimetal carries an electric contactor that makes or breaks the circuit of an electric motor. Because the contactor functions with only two positions, ON and OFF, this system would be categorized as of the on-off type. The motor feeds oil into a boiler, the burning oil heats the water, and hot water or steam is then pumped into the radiators of the rooms to be heated. These constitute the *motor device* and *energy source* of the system. Note that while the energy involved in heating the bimetal is small, very large electric power resources can be brought into play on making the electric contact. This and Fig. 2 illustrate one of the

---

* A bimetal strip is made up of two different metals bonded together. Because the two metals have different temperature expansion coefficients, the bimetal will bend when heated, thus causing the contact to switch on the system. As the strip cools, it straightens and contact is terminated.

major features of control systems concerned with *amplification* of signals from sensor devices. But we have not yet brought into the picture the important element of *feedback*.

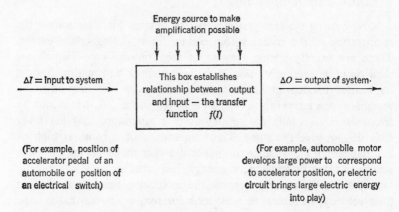

Fig. 2. How a small *input* change (such as the operation of an electric switch) can bring into play sources of energy and thereby produce an *output* that may be quite different in form and magnitude from the input. Each such conversion can be referred to as involving a transformation (transfer function or transform function).

Figure 3 illustrates the sequence of events that occur in our on-off control system where the thermostat is set to hold the temperature of the room at 72° F. Theoretically this might imply that as soon as the temperature falls the slightest bit below 72° F., the thermostat moves to turn on the fuel supply and the boilers, and turns them off again when the temperature returns to 72° F. This would make the system rather too sensitive and erratic, however. Instead, the thermostat is designed to have a *dead zone* of one or a few degrees, within which the temperature may vary without causing motor action. Otherwise vibration, doors opening and closing, and children running would make the control system erratic. Most control systems incorporate a "dead zone" even at the cost of sensitivity and accuracy of control. In Fig. 3 the thermostat turns the heat on at 1° F. below the set control point and turns it off at 1° F. above the set point.

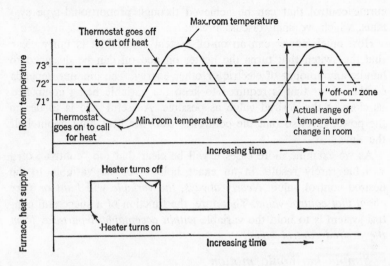

Fig. 3. Relation of room temperature and thermostat to the power input of a room-temperature control system. (From *Introduction to Natural Science.* Courtesy of Academic Press)

The sequence of Fig. 3 starts with the temperature dropping (the upper curve in the figure). When the temperature reaches the lower edge of the differential temperature zone (71° F. in Fig. 3), the thermostat switch makes contact and the motor begins to function. There will usually be some time delay in the response of the thermostat or the motor controls. Because the radiators around the room take minutes to heat up, the temperature of the air in the room continues to drop until it reaches some point well below the lower limit of the control range (about 70° in Fig. 3).

As the heated radiators begin to heat the air in the room, the temperature at the thermostat starts to climb again, and at 73° F. the motors are turned off. But by that time the radiators are fully hot, and the air in the room continues to receive heat and to rise to a temperature well above 73° F. The net result is that the room temperature may vary as much as four or more degrees Fahrenheit with on-off controls. Nevertheless, the simplicity and relatively low cost of on-off systems make them very attractive for many uses. Biological and some social systems, as well as many industrial, mechanical, and chemical processes, usually require the more accurate control that can be achieved through proportional-type systems, which we shall discuss presently.

How much power can an on-off system control? It is fairly clear that the switch that turns the heater on and off can be designed to handle any amount of electric or other energy. The amount depends on the power that is required to keep the variable being controlled as close to the desired value as possible. A useful rule is to design the power level so that the controller calls for heat only about half the time.

As we examine more cases it will be clear that the "control" of a variable rarely results in an exact holding of the variable to the desired control value. *Nearly always, the variable will hunt or vary about that control value.* Therefore, the function of a successful control system is to hold the variable *within acceptable departures from the desired control value.*

Simple harmonic motion

The attractive wave form of temperature variations (or hunting) of Fig. 3 is representative of fluctuations that are experienced by many variables in nature and in human affairs. It is also the very motion that one observes, called simple harmonic motion (or SHM), when a mass is suspended from a coil spring and the up and down movements of the mass are recorded on a paper roll (Fig. 4).

When the bob of Fig. 4 is at rest, its marker will be in the zero position. When we add energy to the system (by raising the bob to some deflection A above the zero line and then releasing it), the bob will drop back and go beyond its zero position to a lower position, as shown. The bob then executes oscillatory motion between the two amplitudes +A and —A.

If we let the marker write on a roll of paper, and pull the paper along while the bob is going up and down, it will draw a curve as shown in Fig. 4 (a). This is the well-known sine curve (or cosine curve), which represents simple harmonic motion and approximates many social phenomena as well.

What observations can we make by watching the bob? Since the bob reverses direction at the upper and lower extremes of the motion, it must be at rest for a very brief instant at each end. At each end of the stroke the bob reverses direction, picks up speed in the new direction, and develops maximum velocity at the instant it passes the zero point (or center point for the stroke). Immediately on passing this center point the bob slows down again so that it comes to rest for an instant at the opposite end of the stroke. The relationships of the velocity and acceleration that accompany the displacement are indicated in Fig. 4.

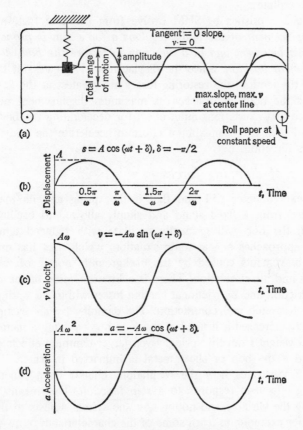

Fig. 4. Equations of simple harmonic motion. (From *Introduction to Natural Science*. Courtesy of Academic Press)

What are the forces that bring about simple harmonic motion? When the bob is still (at the zero position), the pull of the spring equals the pull of gravity. When we pull the bob down by hand, we increase the stretch of the spring and the spring pulls upward with increased force to equal the pull of our hand. We will thereby also have added energy (potential energy in this case) to the system. The increased upward force will now accelerate the mass of the bob, according to Newton's second law, and the potential energy is transformed into kinetic energy and back again to potential energy as the system oscillates.

The characteristics of SHM evolve from this one fact, namely, that *displacement of the body develops a force that is proportional to the displacement and in a direction to restore the body to zero-displacement position.* Since the displacement is greatest at the two ends of the motion, the restoring forces are greatest at the two ends also. As the body approaches its maximum displacement position, this force first exerts maximum effort for decelerating the body to a halt, and then exerts maximum effort to accelerate the body in the opposite direction.

Effect of damping forces

The experimenter will find that if the spring and its mass are suspended from a fixed stand and simply allowed to oscillate untouched, the bob will gradually oscillate with reduced amplitude until it approaches a near-static situation, which then has only the erratic movements caused by the background "noise" of table vibrations and air circulation. There is a little *damping* of the motion by air friction and by frictional heating losses within the spring itself with each stretch and contraction. The damping by air friction can be greatly increased if instead of the solid bob we hang a metal sheet of equal weight from the spring. Even larger damping effects can be observed if the bob or sheet metal is immersed in water.

Fig. 5 illustrates how the oscillations change as a function of damping effects in response to a *step function*. This means simply changing the variable and noting how the system adjusts to the new value. For example, to learn some of the characteristics of an electric circuit we can change a voltage applied to the circuit by some amount and observe how the meter pointer goes to the new value. If there is little damping in the circuit the pointer may overshoot a few times before settling down to the new value (case 1 of Fig. 5). If the damping is severe (case 3 of Fig. 5) the pointer will crawl very slowly to the final value without any overshoot. For quickest

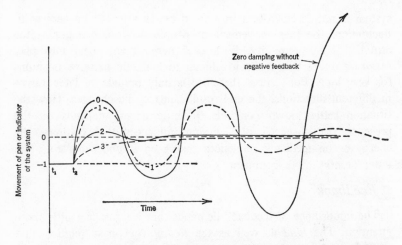

Fig. 5. Effects of damping in a moving system. The moving element (for example a weight on a spring, the pen of a recorder, voltage, etc.) is displaced at time t_1, then at time t_2 it is allowed to return. With some damping (case 1) the system oscillates with reduced amplitude and settles down. With more damping (case 2) it settles down with only a slight overshoot. Heavy damping (case 3) causes the element to slowly crawl to the final position without any overshoot. When damping is absent, however, (case 0) the system does not settle down and may go out of control.

reading, there is incorporated enough damping to overshoot just slightly and to settle back without much more movement (case 2, Fig. 5). Note, however, the behavior of the system when there is no net damping influence (case 0 of Fig. 5). The system not only continues to oscillate, but the amplitude of oscillations may even increase as unusual feedback or "noise" conditions interfere with the stability of the system.

Although the damping just described helps to reduce oscillations, it is usually necessary to introduce negative feedback influences to stabilize control systems.

Non-mechanical systems may experience oscillations similar to simple harmonic motion and for the same reasons. In a socioeconomic system we might identify energy with the activities of individuals who make up a community, and the mass or inertia with the existing pattern of life and activity of the community. When the system is not forcibly held in a fixed position it will be subject to fluctuations, be they movement of people or even changes in the attitude of a community. With each surge there come into play *restoring forces* that make it difficult to maintain extreme positions for very long. Each surge therefore is only prelude to later surges in different directions, the end result being cyclic changes. How the situation settles down (or fails to settle down) depends on the presence (or absence) of damping influences that dissipate the energy or on feedback influences that keep it under control. The latter deserve more comment.

Feedback

The importance of feedback demands that we give it a little more attention. The *kind* as well as the *timing* (or phase relationship) of feedback are rather important. In the case of temperature controllers the thermostat movements find response in heat energy being sent to the room, the feedback finally reaching the neighborhood of the thermostat in the form of heat. The blind person, on the other hand, receives signals in the form of noise and touch, which he converts mentally to transform them into negative feedback in the context of his particular system. For proper control, the feedback must always be *negative*. That is, since the falling temperature initiated action that brought more heat and rising temperature, the feedback must oppose this and reduce the heat input. When a politician approaches his voting constituents on an important issue, he looks for their reactions, or for some form of "feedback." When the response from the audience is encouraging (positive feedback) he may become bolder in his statements or policies, whereas a "negative" feedback is likely to make him more cautious.

Figure 6 illustrates how a feedback function is added to the input-output conversion function that was illustrated in Fig. 2. Feedback may take many forms and many types of coupling. In this illustration some of the output energy is fed back to the input. The box marked FEEDBACK TRANSFER FUNCTION determines how much of, and in what form, the output will be fed back. The input is represented by an arrow with positive increment, while the feedback is shown as an arrow with negative value. In such a setup the net input is *reduced* by the amount of the negative feedback, the effect being to

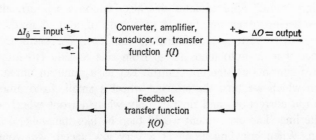

Fig. 6. Addition of a feedback transfer function to the transform function of Fig. 3. (From *Introduction to Natural Science.* Courtesy of Academic Press)

restrain, or limit, the output. If the sign of the feedback were positive, the input and the feedback would add, and the output would increase continually and build up to destruction or to the limit of the energy input. A system with feedback is often referred to as a *closed-loop system.* When used as an energy amplifier, since such systems incorporate a measure of self-correction, the exact value for the amplification becomes less critical, although very high values for gain in amplifiers or control circuits tend to make a system unstable. For this reason high-gain amplifiers especially require negative feedback to stabilize the systems.

We see, therefore, that for a system to be *stable,* the relationship of the forces and time characteristics must be such as to limit the amplitude of fluctuations. This calls for special attention with respect to the *phase relationships* that obtain where feedback of energy from one part of the system to another is concerned. When the *feedback opposes* the direction of the initial change that produced the feedback, the system tends to be *stable.* In contrast, when the returning *feedback* of energy *supports* the direction of initial change, the system tends to add to the initial energy gain and to be *unstable.* This appears to suggest that during an argument a husband and wife should avoid raising voices at the same time.

Driving an automobile

The system we described for controlling the temperature of a room falls in the on-off category. That is, the thermostat contactor either makes or breaks contact to complete the motor circuitry.

Walking "blind" approximates this also. Suppose we turn attention to the driving of an automobile in a lane of a road marked with white lines to restrict movements to the lane. We know from experience that an auto tends to go from side to side (to hunt) and requires continuous steering control. Let us assume an unreal situation in which we turn the steering wheel a small, fixed amount to make the correction, and do this only when a front wheel touches a white line. The experiment would then be like the walk of a blind person. When crawling along at a very low speed, we would find that the car does not go very much outside the lane, but when driving at moderate speeds this type of correction (applying a fixed amount of adjustment as in on-off control) causes the car to weave in and out of the lane substantially. If we were to drive even faster, the car would be likely to leave the road altogether. The amount of overshoot would depend on how slowly we respond to visual signals and take action.

Fortunately not many people drive in this manner, because control of an automobile utilizes a much more sophisticated system of elements than is possible with on-off control. In fact, not many automatic industrial processes can compare with the sophistication and effectiveness of good auto driving, since human judgment enters this operation to a remarkable degree. To begin with, the driver is kept continually informed of each new situation through his sense of sight and general physical awareness. (There is continuous feedback, or information, reaching him to guide his next move.) The element of judgment or experience also enters. He can vary the sharpness of turn of the steering wheel to conform to the sharp right turn. This is called *proportional control*. In addition, because he can see a curve in the road ahead long before the auto reaches the curve he can anticipate the move (*anticipatory control*) and thus reduce delay in his action (Fig. 7).

The driver of an automobile is aware of several conditions that make control more difficult. If the steering wheel has looseness, or "play," in the shaft or gear system, the steering wheel must be turned several degrees of angle before there is any effect on the front-wheel direction. This play, or region of no response, is sometimes called the *dead zone* of the system. The driver himself may be a little slow in judging the situation and taking action. This "lag," or slowness of response, together with looseness in the steering system, can make for wider overshoot in the movement of the car. If the throttle sticks or the motor hesitates or the brakes seize, the

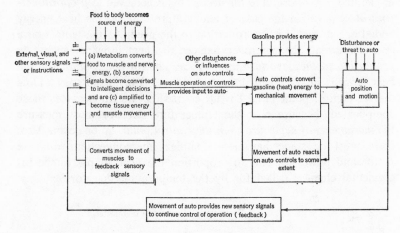

Fig. 7. The input, output, energy-source, and feedback influences that bear on the driving of an automobile. (From *Introduction to Natural Science.* Courtesy of Academic Press)

driver will not be able to assure smooth "feel" and ride. Finally, roughness of the road can introduce random fluctuations that add uncertainty to the normal small feedback of information. A driver is not likely to give delicate guidance to the auto when his whole body is being shaken. This background confusion is often called *noise,* or *static,* when one is referring to transmission of a signal or of information. It exists in almost every type of control circuit, sometimes in the form of vibration of an automobile or plant equipment. It occurs in the normal radioactivity background of the environment, which disturbs radiation measurements. In very sensitive electronic circuitry it shows up in the random movements of the electrons. Similar phenomena are present in social situations and in biological organisms that maintain balance in their internal functions and with their environment.

Characteristics of proportional control

From the example of driving an automobile we see that the on-off type of control, in which the action taken is in fixed steps (full on and full off), is inadequate for many applications that require closer control. Undesirable surges can be reduced if the action taken is moderated *in proportion to the need*. This is achieved in *proportional-control systems*. In the case of temperature control, the heat energy added or subtracted is in proportion to the need. As the temperature rises somewhat, the controller reduces the heat input somewhat *in proportion to the departure from the set control point*. Similarly, the heat input is increased in proportion to a fall in temperature below the set control point (Fig. 8). Of course the system becomes more complicated, because now the temperature detector must measure the *increments of departure from the control point*, up or down. Also, there must be somewhat more complex interconnection with the motor and power systems to proportion the heat supply to the incremental changes called for by the temperature detector.

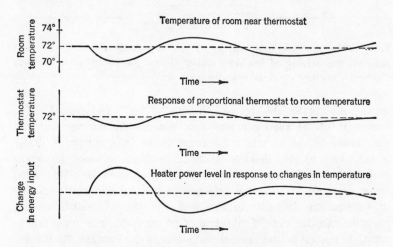

Fig. 8. In a proportional-control system, the response of the thermostat is proportional to the departure of room temperature from the desired control point, and the change in power input to the boiler is proportional to the response of the thermostat. (From *Introduction to Natural Science*. Courtesy of Academic Press)

There is, however, a serious limitation in proportional-control systems when the load demand changes so that a different average power level must be applied to hold the variable at the desired control value. To understand this, we note that in proportional control, the output ΔO (Fig. 2) has a fixed ratio to the input ΔI. This proportionality ratio, or gain, may be represented by $G=\Delta O/\Delta I$. Assume that the room-temperature control we have been discussing is set to control at 72° F. *when the outdoor temperature is around 50° F.* We may assume that this requires an average heat input of 10,000 Btu* per hour. Suppose that the outdoor temperature drops to zero F. Obviously, the heater system must provide a great deal more heat to hold the temperature at 72° F.— say, 30,000 Btu per hour. We therefore need an additional 20,000 Btu per hour (30,000—10,000) to hold the temperature at 72° F. But since in proportional control more heat is provided only in proportion to the temperature drop from the control setting, how can the additional heat be provided without the actual temperature remaining well below the desired control value?

Let us analyze the situation a little more quantitatively. Suppose the gain of our control is set so that, for each degree that the temperature drops, the controller permits an additional 2000 Btu per hour to be supplied to the boiler. This represents a gain, or proportionality, ratio of 2000 Btu per hour per degree Fahrenheit. To get the additional 20,000 Btu would require that the temperature of the room go down to 62° F. Or alternatively, the thermostat setting would have to be moved arbitrarily to about 80° F. in order to supply enough heat to hold the room temperature at 72° F. as long as the outdoor temperature remained at zero.

This discrepancy could be reduced if the gain were made higher (that is, 1° F. could turn on much more than an additional 2000 Btu per hour). But making the gain higher also makes the system more unstable. Other devices can be introduced to change the responsiveness of the controller, such as incorporating into the system an outdoor thermostat that introduces the equivalent of an arbitrary shift of the thermostat setting to 80° F. We need not go into more detail beyond recognizing this severe limitation of proportional-control systems.

The closed-loop amplifier system

Fig. 9 illustrates in a more formal way a closed-loop amplifier system in which an input signal E_i (which may be in volts and

---

* The British thermal unit is the amount of heat required to raise the temperature of one pound of water one degree Fahrenheit.

related to temperature, pressure, blood count, or other variable) constitutes the control variable. The system may be designed to do something that is proportional to or determined by this control variable. If the system is a servomechanism, input E_i may represent the angle of rotation of a small motor, and output E_o the angle of rotation of a larger motor, the objective being to keep the two motors in step with each other. Or E_i may be the input voltage from a measuring circuit that has high resistance and low power and is to be converted to an identical voltage in a low-resistance circuit to operate a loudspeaker or solenoid or some other device that requires more power than is available at the input end of the circuit. (Throughout this discussion keep in mind that there must be a source of energy to make this conversion possible, as is illustrated in Fig. 9.)

The signal E_i may have a fixed value or may vary with time. It feeds into a comparator element, where E_i is compared (added) to the signal coming as feedback. If the input signal and the feedback are equal (equal amounts of positive input and of negative feedback cancel each other), there remains zero *error; conversely, if they are not equal, a difference signal* will be fed to the amplifier or transducer. The output of the amplifier goes through a unit that represents all the undesirable disturbances (E_D) that can upset the balance. These may be a sudden twist of the output shaft in the case

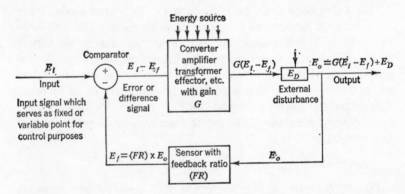

Fig. 9. A closed-loop amplifier system. (From *Introduction to Natural Science*. Courtesy of Academic Press)

of the servomotor, a sudden drop in temperature when a new load of cold metal is injected into an industrial melting furnace, or a sudden bend of the body that changes blood-pressure requirements. As the disturbance changes the motor position, temperature, or blood pressure, there automatically develops also a change in the feedback loop. The feedback and input E_i are then no longer in balance, and the sudden error signal that results from the imbalance causes the amplifier to go into action to restore balance.

By way of review

For a summary of this chapter let us list the functional elements that make up most control systems:

First there is the *variable* that the system is expected to cope with or to control within prescribed limits. Actually it is rare that only one variable is present in a system. In the case of room-temperature control, the changes in the outdoor temperature constitute an *independent variable,* while the internal temperature represents the *controlled variable.* Other independent variables may be introduced, such as children running in and out of doors.

Similarly, the driver of the automobile has control devices by which he steers and starts and stops the car in relation to the road. But all along the way he is forced to comply with independent demands such as those made by changing road and traffic conditions, stop signs, and traffic lights, all of which constitute independent variables.

Usually there must be *sensor devices,* by which changes in the variable can be measured or detected. In the case of temperature measurement, a thermostat usually includes a bimetal that carries an electrical contact; the bimetal changes its position when the air temperature changes and thus makes or breaks an electric circuit. Similarly, while the position and speed of the automobile are the variables to be controlled, we gauge these by the use of sensory information (vision, hearing) and the interpretive processes of the brain. The economist also looks for meaningful indexes by which to gauge the larger features of the national product, industrial trends, and public attitudes. The public has its own measures for gauging quality and values.

Whether one deals with a temperature-control system, driving an automobile, or any other situation that involves variables and controls, there must be a *source of energy* by which the job is performed.

In most instances the sensory function makes use of the services of a *motor device* to utilize energy that restores the variable to its proper value. In the temperature-control system, the blowers and burners (which are triggered into action by the thermostat) begin to utilize fuel energy to heat the boilers. In the automobile a number of mechanisms come into play to burn the gasoline, to power the steering, and to perform other non-driver functions.

Finally there is a feedback device, or *feedback function,* which in one way or another relates the output to the input and thus controls the net output.

Even if individual parts of a system cannot be identified specifically with these five functions, they are present in one form or another. There can be a wide variety of transformations (*transform functions*) even in electromechanical systems: Molecular energy bends a bimetal, which in turn completes an electric circuit that starts motors and oil pumps. Oil burns in a boiler to produce heat, which is transported to another area by other motor devices. Similarly, many tangible and intangible features of human physical energy and human brain processes become involved in driving an automobile.

In general we may say the following about control systems:

(1) Stable control requires the presence of negative feedback influences.

(2) Stable control of a variable to a "fixed" point usually means maintaining the variable so that it does not hunt beyond acceptable limits around the point.

(3) To be effective for the control of any variable, the control system must be designed to have response rates that are suited to the specific application.

These and other characteristics of control systems will be illustrated in subsequent chapters. But now we must give attention to the neurological system of the body and the key role it plays in the control of body processes.

CHAPTER 5

Neurological Functions of the Body

"A pencil of light from the sun enters the eye and is focused there on the retina. It gives rise to a change, which in turn travels to the nerve-layer at the top of the brain. The whole chain of these events, from the sun to the top of my brain, is physical. Each step is an electrical reaction. But now there succeeds a change wholly unlike any which led up to it, and wholly inexplicable by us."*

Sherrington

The discussions of the previous chapter progressed from measurements one can make on individually visible objects to measurements of thermodynamic, secondary effects of particles that are invisibly small and yet so numerous and active as to have overpowering consequences on natural processes. For example, the freezing temperatures that characterize declining motion of molecules can have far more devastating effects on a region of lands and lakes than a single large object is likely to produce. But even these phenomena cannot vie with the subtleties that come into power when the mind of man takes over the control of energy, of matter, and of fellow men. To appreciate this we have only to recall such things as the invention of nuclear bombs, or the domination of Hitlerlike demagogues and dictators.

But the subject must begin with a simpler introduction to the brain and to neurological phenomena, for which purpose the experience of the quotation that introduces this chapter is particularly suited. That

* C. Sherrington, in his introduction to *The Physical Basis of Mind*, edited by P. Laslett (New York: The Macmillan Co., 1950). © Macmillan Co.

is, before we enter the realm of mental processes we must pass through an intermediate zone that transforms motion of physical particles and of electric charges into useful sensory signals.

Sherrington's "pencil of light" suddenly becomes a magnificent panorama of sky and sun "and a hundred other visual things besides," of mental images, concepts, relationships. The chain of events does not stop even there, however, for these constitute only the beginning of unique response-and-control phenomena. The subtlety of the experience might well evoke the reactions expressed by Sherrington: ". . . I ought, I suppose, to feel startled, but I am too accustomed to feel even surprised." For only after extensive research do we learn that no industrial or laboratory controls can match the body's systems for sensitivity, small size, adaptability to varied conditions, longevity, and over-all effectiveness. These, and especially the role of the brain, as parts of "cybernetic systems" constitute the theme for this and the next two chapters.

The role of the neural system

In this article "Why Do We Laugh?" the philosopher Henri Bergson recites the plight of the man who, running down the street, stumbles and falls and thereby becomes the object of laughing ridicule. The cause of the fall may have been a stone on the road. Bergson reasons that it was the involuntary element in his sudden change of posture, which smacked of clumsiness, that brought on the laughter. He should have added that the act appeared clumsy because although the man was well equipped with sensory and motor control capabilities to meet the situation without incident, he failed to take advantage of his capabilities. A blind person tripping and falling would not elicit the same response from onlookers, even though the involuntary element and clumsiness might be present to an equal degree. To a considerable degree we evaluate an act on the basis of how easy or difficult it is to perform it in view of the performer's natural capabilities. We applaud when an animal plays *Yankee Doodle* on horns but would be quite dismayed if an adult human performer were limited to the same act. We condemn a person for making statements that appear foolish when "he should have known better" through means available to him.

Clumsiness, mishaps, and embarrassment would be rather common to all of us were it not for the facility with which nature endowed us for responding to our environment. The information-gathering and information-utilizing processes of the body vary enormously. The "sources" of information are sometimes within the body as response to hunger or pain, but more often they arise as response to activities outside the body. The experience may involve heavy muscular effort, with large expenditure of energy and a minimum of informational content, as when one must push an obstacle out of the way of his vehicle. On another occasion the physical force and energy content may be negligible in relation to the *informational aspects* of the experience, as when one reads an interesting book. In any case, while every sensorimotor experience involves physical quantities that we have identified as energy, force, and mass, the physical quantities are now accompanied by subtleties that we call *information, thinking, perception.*

With sensory-control processes in mind it is useful to identify the organizational and functional capabilities of a living organism in three categories: There are, first, the internal biochemical processes whereby the organism obtains energy and substance from food intake. These include the regulation of processes in which the individual cell is a participant and the regulation of the larger tissues and organs and fluids that make up the body. We can call these the *internal organismic functions,* in the context of our present interest.

Since an organism can survive only if it maintains an adequate biological interrelationship and balance with its immediate environment, we may refer to *interrelationship with environment* as the second aspect with respect to neurological functions. Most of the phenomena accompanying the feeding and protection of an organism, as well as genetic and procreative processes, might be included in this category. The sensorimotor functions of the plant world can usually be limited to these two categories.

As we probe into the activities of the animal world and especially of man's society there must be assigned a third category, which we might call the *sociological and cultural level.* Interrelationships with environment take on new dimensions and very subtle forms. Small and large animals develop a sense of fear and of safety, and we never cease to wonder at the craving for affection that appears in so many animal species. The human species develop social structures, thinking and reasoning processes, language and communication processes, patterns of logic, new food and mating habits, population explosions, intense religious and political experiences, idealism with intolerance, cultural and social codes that on occasion sacrifice the biological needs of the body and life itself. The simpler, sensorimotor activities provide a logical basis for systematic knowledge, which in turn brings new social capabilities and new cultural patterns; but from time to time there emerge emotional outbursts in the form of new political ideologies, new religious fervor, and new youth rebellion to demonstrate how inadequate the "systematic knowledge" really is.

While most of the mechanisms that effect these transformations are inexplicable, there is value in trying to identify some of them through neurological features that are observable in our own body functions.

Some observations on the breathing function

We note first the *rhythmic,* cyclic character of breathing and of heart action, which go on automatically, independently of any thinking on our part. From observation of the accompanying muscle action that expands and contracts the entire thoracic cage, we sense that many muscle tissues work *in concert.* Since we know that muscle tissue is made up of very large numbers of tiny muscle cells, we judge that to produce action in concert there exists a very *extensive system of nerve fibers that interconnect the cells.*

We can, of course, control the periodicity and depth of breathing to produce precise speech or song or to play a difficult wind instrument. This suggests that rhythmic controls can be overridden by *controls associated with the highest levels of the nervous system,* which we shall see to be in the cerebral cortex. One immediate inference is that when voluntary control takes over, concurrently some *inhibitory function* prevents the automatic control mechanism from interfering. Note, however, that as one holds the breath, voluntary control must periodically give way to the primary function of the lungs, which is to keep the body processes in balance by receiving adequate oxygen and dispelling carbon dioxide. That is, there seem to be limiting controls that are sensitive to the oxygen demands and the carbon-dioxide concentrations of the body, and that take over against voluntary control. Moreover, new controls seem to dominate the breathing function whenever unusual effort or exercise makes heavier demands for oxygen or for the exhaustion of carbon dioxide.

With a little more attention, we presently become aware of the

smoothness of the breathing function even as the body passes from one body condition to another. Finally, there is a close reciprocal relationship between the mental and physical condition of the body and the breathing process. A disturbed state of body induces irregularity in the breathing, while smooth, regular, somewhat voluntarily controlled breathing can help to produce calm in the body.*
This integration and co-ordination must be attributed to the presence of an extensive system of communication among the cells and parts of the body, the "communication" being possibly as often inhibitory as initiative.

The gastrointestinal system

Several times a day we experience hunger. There is some regularity in the time of day when the hunger pangs occur, as though directed by a "biological clock" within the body. When we take food, or even disregard the hunger pangs, the demand for food ceases until the time for the next meal approaches.

When we do take food, a complex chain of responses is set into operation with automatic regularity. Almost at once the salivary glands secrete saliva, which helps the swallowing and digestion of food. The secretion may be initiated by the presence of food or by the mechanical action of the jaws. On the other hand, mental processes such as the recollection of a particular food can also initiate secretion. We guess that the higher nerve centers may substitute sensory sensations that are normally provided by other sensors, such as by taste receptors in the mouth.

Following intake of food, the digestive processes of the body seem to proceed with automatic regularity except when the influence of extreme anxiety, fear, anger, or fatigue renders the food unpalatable and even upsetting. Conversely, moderate emotions of anxiety as well as the sight of food can elicit feelings of hunger.†

---

* This reciprocal relationship of breathing regularity and bodily calm can be readily demonstrated by anyone who is familiar with the principles of yogic exercises.
† The reader can pursue this theme with such books as *Biology and Behavior: Neurophysiology and Emotion,* proceedings of a conference under the auspices of the Russell Sage Foundation and The Rockefeller University, David C. Glass, editor (New York: The Rockefeller University Press, 1967).

The sensory system

The senses of touch, vision, hearing, smell, and taste involve receptor organs (skin, eyes, ears, nose, and tongue) that are clearly quite different from one another. The kinds of information that the brain derives from them also differ one from another, and probably all our experiences with the outside world utilize information that the senses offer in combination. Thus when we look at a tree, an automobile, or an apple, what we perceive is not just what the eyes see. Perception involves much more. We "see" also the results of earlier experiences that came with touching, hearing, smelling, or tasting other objects that are related in some way to the objects that are presently in view. In fact we may "see" things that may not be there at all in the present instance. Thus every current sensory experience is enriched by previous experiences. By the same token we must admit that every present sensory experience is distorted and biased by the experiences that preceded it.

When the body is in a state of calm and rest, the sensory system is more capable of receiving weak sensory signals, whereas fatigue or pain stimuli make it difficult to receive weak sensory stimuli or to undertake carefully controlled muscular movements. We realize all too often how difficult it is to hold tongue and temper when there is fatigue or pain. It is also possible to make the sensory system more sensitive, as when fingers are trained to become highly sensitive to the feel of objects, and taste buds become more selective of differences in wines or foods. Even the delay time between the instant a sensory stimulus is received and the time when muscles go into action can be reduced by training the system to be more receptive and responsive to certain signals—for example, when driving an automobile. Most of us also learn that sensory sensitivity and muscle control are impaired when the body is under the influence of alcohol or of drugs.

In any case, the sensory system takes the physical input derived from the environment and converts this in the form of a vast number of sensations or "bits"* of sensations to the nervous system and the

---

* When we discuss nerve discharges, we shall refer to "bits" of information, where the word "bit" as used in information theory is a contraction of the term *binary digit*.

brain. The latter must accept, integrate, and ascribe meaning to the sensations according to immediate or earlier experiences. As we shall note presently, many of the integrative functions take place automatically, utilizing only the extensive neural interconnections within the neural system other than the cortex. But the nervous system is capable of higher *associative* functions as well, such as the ability to interpret the significance of sensations, to think, to originate ideas, and to activate functions called for by various situations. These associative functions are among the least understood of physiological phenomena. They are also the most intriguing, because they relate to our learning processes, and we may assume that better understanding of the functions of the brain could lead to tremendous advances in the process of learning and perhaps of thinking.

These, then, are among the observations and experiences for which we must find explanations in the workings of the nervous system. Before searching for explanations, however, it will be useful to place these observations within the framework of *control systems of the body,* for indeed the main features of neurological phenomena are best revealed within such a framework; that is, the importance of the phenomena we have noted as sensory information and as muscle action and co-ordination lies in the aid they give the body "to do something." The "doing something" may be jumping out of the way of an oncoming vehicle, taking nourishment, making love, or anything else. Whatever its nature, the total act usually has aspects of a control system that includes *information* as *feedback*. For that reason we take a few minutes to note the significance of the *control functions* that are attributed to living organisms.

The need for control functions (*homeostasis, homeodynamics*)

The proper sustenance of an organism requires that equilibrium conditions be maintained with its environment and within the organism itself. Equilibrium conditions are not maintained automatically or easily, however, because the environmental, socioeconomic, and sociopolitical factors that bear down on man are more often unfavorable than favorable for maintaining balance. The biochemical processes through which the organism derives energy from food are exceedingly complex and easily disrupted. Or as Émile

Souvestre expressed it, "The stomach is a slave that must accept everything that is given to it, but which avenges wrongs as slyly as does the slave." We can also point to larger examples of imbalance in the world, wherein large numbers of people are overnourished and very many more are undernourished, all living in the same world environment.

How are mammals and birds able to maintain a fairly constant internal body temperature despite exposure to temperatures that may range from $-31°$ F. to values that exceed the boiling point of water ($212°$ F.) for short periods? In man the temperature of the blood remains very close to $98.6°$ F. ($37°$ C.) despite exposure of the body to wide changes in environmental temperature and humidity. The need for answers to such questions was probably first recognized by the French physiologist Claude Bernard (1813–78). Bernard abandoned a faltering career as an author and playwright to go into medicine. By 1843 he had acquired his degree with especial interest in physiology, in which he achieved much-greater fame.

In his book *Introduction to the Study of Experimental Medicine,* published in 1865, Bernard explored the reasons for the *constancy of the internal environment* of the body. He saw this constancy, or fixedness, of the *"milieu intérieur"* as of the very essence of life. He studied the functions of gastric juices in the metabolism of the body, the functions of the liver, the constancy of body temperature, and the control of blood flow rates through the dilating and constricting action of vessels stimulated by vasomotor nerves. For example, the extracellular fluid that surrounds each cell of the body is surprisingly constant in its composition, whether the body is overfed or starving, whether the external environment is hot or cold, and regardless of the variations in diet to which the body may be subject. Altogether, the evidence seems to indicate that the constancy of the internal environment is a necessary condition for good health. In an age when many of the body's functions were attributed to "animal spirits," Bernard succeeded in extending to the study of the body the logic of "cause and effect" that had developed with Newtonian mechanics.

Others sought explanations for the body's ability to bring into play functions that effectively resist wide departures from equilibrium. The Belgian physiologist Léon Frederic, in 1885 declared:

"The living being is an agency of such sort that each disturbing influence induces by itself the calling forth of compensatory activity to neutralize or repair the disturbance. The higher in the scale of living beings, the more perfect and the more complicated do these regulatory agencies become."

It was an American physiologist at Harvard Medical School, Walter B. Cannon, who in the course of a very productive lifetime (1871–1945) made a detailed analysis of some of the control and restoration processes of the body. He utilized X-ray penetration to study the behavior of the stomachs of cats—the rhythmic motions that accompany swallowing, digestion, and elimination. He followed the sudden changes in stomach behavior that develop when the cat is alarmed, and the accompanying increase of rate of heartbeat and cessation of gastric secretion that prepare its full energies to meet emergencies.

Cannon was so impressed with the tendency of the body always to return to its stable state and for the extracellular fluids to retain their constancy of composition that he coined the word *homeostasis** to describe this tendency. While the word has become quite common, it fails to give a correct impression of the dynamic character of the control activities that make this stability or constancy possible. For this reason another term, *homeokinesis,* has been suggested. The term *homeodynamics* is even more appropriate for control operations that are sometimes simple, sometimes complex, but always dynamic.

These, then, are personal observations for which we must seek explanations in the anatomy and physiology of the nervous system. There are contained within that scope the very same functional elements that we have associated with other, more mechanical cybernetic systems, namely sensory means, motor means, energy sources, feedback influences, information, and capabilities for processing and interrelating these toward "goals" of various kinds.

The neural system

How can we offer some indication of the complexity of the neurological or communication system of a single human being? Picture

* *Homeo*=like or similar; *stasis*=a standing, stoppage, or retardation.

the vast network of power-generation, power-utilization, and communication facilities that supply over 200 million individuals of the United States. For our purposes we can assume that they are served by several hundred power-generating stations, several hundred large city centers, roughly 100 million telephones, and vast numbers of electric-power and telephone lines. There are heavy power lines and telephone trunk lines that connect the cities, each trunk line made up of thousands of wires connecting to telephone instruments in individual homes. Each house may be pictured as having its own temperature-control system. The national picture represents a very complex system. Yet a comparison with the human body requires that we multiply that total complexity many times. For example, the nervous system of the body contains more than 10 billion neurons, or nerve cells, most of them being in the brain.

A single neuron of the cerebral cortex may be so interconnected as to influence the behavior of a hundred other cell bodies. This suggests that the interconnections (through synapses, which we shall presently discuss) between neurons may number around 1000 billion. They lead from sensory receptors of the five kinds we have named to dozens more kinds that we cannot even name. There are receptors that are sensitive to concentrations of salt or hydrogen ions, pressure, oxygen, carbon dioxide, sugars, enzymes, secretions of many kinds.

The comparison of nerve fibers with the lines of a telephone circuit is not altogether unfitting, for as we shall presently see, communication through nerve fibers is also by means of electrical pulses.

The principal means for communicating information or awareness from one part of the body to another part is the neural cell, or *neuron*. Like most other cells of the body, the neuron has a nucleus inside the cytoplasm. Unlike other cells, however, neurons tend to be elongated and to vary greatly in size and geometry and in their interrelationship. It is difficult to identify a "typical" neuron. Neurons are polarized in the sense that each one has an *input end*, the *dendrites*, through which it is sensitized to receive an electric pulse, and an *output end*, the *axon*, through which it sends the pulse to other cells. One form is shown in Fig. 10. The dendritic, or receiving, zones are usually made up of many hairlike fibers resembling the branches of a tree, while the transmitting, or axon, ends are also branched to some extent, with each branch ending in a bulb or button. The axon end may vary in length from a few microns to great lengths—as much as several meters in some cases. (A micron is one millionth of a meter.)

The nucleus of the neuron is surrounded by a metabolic envelope, or "center," where the protein required for the neuron is synthesized, the combination being called the perikaryon.* While many other cells of the body undergo mitosis, or cell division, neurons rarely do, but they are among the most active cells of the body in synthesizing substances for their own normal use.†

As we have noted, each neuron has a receiving end and an output end; the neurons are classified according to the organ from which they receive signals and the organ or tissue to which they transmit signals: *Receptor neurons* receive (or generate) signals at sensory organs such as the skin, eyes, or ears, and transmit these signals to other neurons of the *central nervous system* (CNS). *Effector neurons* receive signals from other neurons within the central nervous system and transmit the signals to the muscle, or motor, elements of the body. The latter are also often called *motoneurons* and sometimes *efferent* neurons. There is a third category, called *interneuron,* which as the name implies, play an intermediary role in connecting one neuron to another neuron. As we shall see, interneurons permit great diversity and integration in the neural network by sometimes connecting many receptor neurons to one or more motoneurons or one receptor neuron to many motoneurons. The tiny interconnecting region where a neuron passes its signal to another neuron is called a *synapse.* Thus a receptor neuron always has its receiving end at a sensory organ where signals are generated from such stimuli as light, heat, touch, smell, and taste, and has its output end at a synapse. An effector neuron usually has its input end at a synapse and its output end at a muscle. Interneurons usually lead from one or more synapses to one or more other synapses.

The uniqueness of the neurons of the three categories lies in the functions that are associated with the *membrane* that envelopes the

---

* Peri=all around, about, beyond, from the Greek; *karyon* is also from the Greek, meaning the nut, kernel, and as used here, the nucleus.

† The reader will find extended discussions of these and of other neurological topics in the volume *The Neurosciences* (see References). For this portion we have drawn from the chapter "Neurons, Circuits, and Neuroglia," by David Bodian.

neurons. The receiving end of receptor neurons must be sensitive to specific environmental changes and respond to such changes by initiating an electric pulse at the receiving (dendrite) end of the neuron. The electric pulse is then carried along the axon either to enter the various nerve centers or to be passed directly on to the input end of effector neurons to effect muscle action. This being the case, each receptor neuron must have input organelles (fibers) that are suitable for the function to be performed. Neurons that receive signals from the eyes have organelles that are sensitive to light energy. Other receptor organs have end organs (and membranes) that respond to mechanical vibrations, heat, touch, and chemical substances. Each receptor generates an electric pulse at the input end that passes via the perikaryon to the axon of the neuron. The axon (Fig. 10) can be quite short or quite long. Its diameter can be very fine (of the order of 0.2 micron) or much larger. Larger axons are likely to be enfolded in multiple, concentric folds of lipid (fatty) membranous material, which constitutes a *myelin sheath,* the fibers then being called *myelinated.*

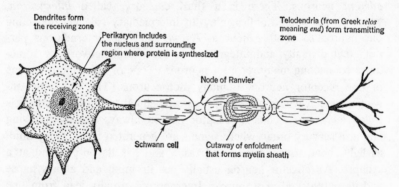

Fig. 10. The neuron, shown with part of an axon enfolded in membranes that form the myelin sheath. In the case of nerves of the central nervous system, there is further enfoldment within a membrane of glial cells, while peripheral nerves have a similar "satellite" relationship with Schwann cells. (From *Introduction to Natural Science.* Courtesy of Academic Press)

Neural interconnections: the synapse

All that *receptor neurons* can do is to pass sensory signals to the central nervous system of the body, while activation of the muscles is entrusted to the *effector neurons.* There must therefore be some form of interconnection for transmitting signals from the receptor neurons to the effector neurons. Let us assume a case in which a single afferent, or receptor, neuron receives stimulation and passes the signal on to an efferent, or effector, neuron that leads directly to muscle tissue. In such a simple case the region of interconnection between the afferent and efferent neurons is called the *synaptic region,* or the *synapse.* Figure 11 (a) illustrates how the axon and *telodendria* of an afferent neuron communicate through protoplasm tissue with the dendrites of an efferent neuron without the two neurons' making direct contact.

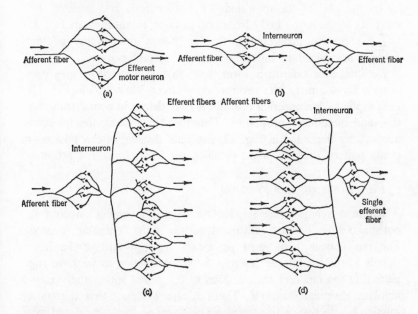

Fig. 11. Representations of neuron interactions that may take place at a synapse. (a) illustrates a simple synapse between an afferent and an efferent nerve. In (b) there is an intermediary neuron (called interneuron) between the entering, afferent nerve and the leaving, efferent nerve fibers. In (c) a neural discharge that enters the synaptic area through a single afferent nerve fiber becomes extended (amplified) to go out to many efferent nerve fibers. In (d) the reverse takes place, with the discharges entering from many neurons and leaving through a single neuron. (From *Introduction to Natural Science.* Courtesy of Academic Press)

Interconnection through a synapse, or synaptic region, offers a number of advantages: It provides means for modifying or integrating the afferent signals before they become action signals to the effector neurons. Or signals may be redirected to the higher nerve centers. Figure 11 (b) shows how an *interneuron* may intervene between an afferent and an efferent neuron. In Figure 11 (c) a single afferent neuron makes connection with a whole series of efferent neurons, so that the pulses generated in the one neuron become extended (magnified) to influence many neurons of the central nervous system. For example, such a *divergent* circuit (sometimes called *internuncial**) permits a single source of neural impulses to initiate concerted activity on the part of the thousands of motoneurons and muscles that must act to move the body from one position to another. In Fig. 11 (d) the reverse takes place; that is, pulses from many afferent neurons are joined to influence a single efferent neuron.

We shall note one other form that synaptic interconnections may provide for—namely, the reverberatory circuit illustrated in Fig. 12. A synaptic interconnection introduces time delays in neural transmission and directional properties. Therefore, by cycling the interconnections as illustrated in Fig. 12, neuronal discharges can take on a cyclic pattern such as might produce rhythmic, repetitive action.

Functions of the synapse

Within a synapse, the telodendria of an "incoming" neuron do not make direct contact with the dendrites of the "outgoing" neuron. For this reason there must be means for transmitting the input signals across the intervening gap. Such information as we have suggests that the mode of transmission of the signal within the synapse involves chemical reactions. There is also evidence that the transmission is selective, with several possibilities: an incoming signal may be transmitted without change, it may be modified, or it may be blocked altogether. This selective response makes the synapse a principal means whereby a course of action is determined. Synaptic connections vary considerably in structure and function. Often the membranes of the two cells come close together but with an inter-

* A comparison of such circuitry with the circuitry of computers will be made in Chapter 7.

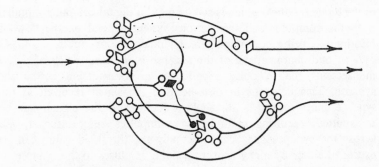

Fig. 12. Example of how neuronal interconnections with feedback can develop a reverberatory circuit. The black neuron represents inhibitory influences.

stitial space of between 150 and 200 Å.* There is likely to be tufted filamentous material in that space. The chemical substance *acetylcholine* is likely to be found there, along with tiny vesicles that are roughly spherical and with diameters of around 200 to 400 Å. Apparently substances that may either excite another neuron or inhibit excitation are secreted at the presynaptic terminals. The activities within the synapse have a great deal to do with the functioning of the entire nervous system. For this reason considerable research has been directed to the study of the synaptic regions of the nervous system.

One of the important features of transmission across the synapse is that it is *unidirectional*. When the axon of a neuron is artificially stimulated along its length, nerve impulses travel in both directions from the point of stimulation. That is, the neuron itself lacks unidirectional properties. However, pulses that travel "backward" toward the input end are not permitted to cross the synapse, whereas pulses traveling in the direction of the axon ending are transmitted through the synapse to the dendrite of another neuron. The flow of nerve impulses in the nervous system therefore produces a unidirectional flow of information. Without such directional control over flow, the behavior of the nervous system would be chaotic indeed.

* An angstrom (Å) equals 10^{-10} meter.

In this property of directional conduction the synapse can be likened to the *diode rectifier,* which is so common in digital computer circuits. Both the computer and the nervous system depend on the flow of information being controlled through unidirectional units.

A second characteristic of the synapse is the *time delay* of a few milliseconds that a pulse experiences in transmission across the synapse. This develops in part because the signal received at the synapse must exceed a threshold value before the signal can be transmitted, requiring multiple nerve impulses before transmission across the synapse can occur. Actually the threshold value can be exceeded either by many neurons sending impulses to the synapse or by one neuron "firing" more than once in quick succession. In any case the synapse "sums up" the over-all input of signals and acts accordingly. The synapse thus has the property of *summation* of signals that reach it, with further action on its part being determined by the nature of the integrated signals. Of course, the summation may be an adding up of inhibitory influences.

The exact mechanism of transmission across the synapse is unclear. Some investigators believe that an electric charge and discharge phenomenon is involved, as at a cell membrane, and that the transmission is due to chemical changes. According to this hypothesis the membrane at the axon ending of a neuron (output end) secretes *acetylcholine,* which depolarizes the surface of the dendrites (input end) of the next neuron and thereby stimulates that neuron. The acetylcholine is then destroyed by an enzyme called *cholinesterase,* found in the same area. Certain nerve gases that have been produced recently are capable of destroying this enzyme. In the absence of the enzyme, the acetylcholine is not destroyed, the membrane remains depolarized, and a form of local paralysis is produced as further conduction of impulses becomes impossible.

The chemical theory of synaptic transmission could account for the experimentally observed time delay in the transmission of impulses across the synapse, since the delay represents the time required to build up adequate amounts of acetylcholine. The delay amounts to about .005 second in the average synapse. Summation could represent the deposition of acetylcholine from successive pulses. However, the phenomenon of inhibition is much more difficult to explain.

A third characteristic of the synapse is that it is very sensitive to the action of drugs, to lack of oxygen, and to fatigue. This characteristic imposes some limitations on nerve-discharge phenomena that are not directly the limitations of nerves or muscles. Studies have shown that when an individual exercises to such a point of exhaustion that his muscles can no longer contract or work under his control, both the nerves leading to these muscles and the muscles themselves will nevertheless respond to direct stimulation; that is, fatigue seems to take place in the synapse rather than within the nerves and muscles.

Synaptic interconnections provide for combinations of neurons into larger functional groupings known as *neuronal pools*. The central nervous system is made up of literally hundreds of separate neuronal pools, some of which are extremely small and some very large. For instance, the entire cerebral cortex could be considered a single large neuronal pool.

The nerve impulse

The functions of the nerve cells and of the neurological system as a whole involve electrical currents and potentials, chemical changes, and possibly pressure changes as well. Of these, the most easily measured are the electric effects, and unfortunately most of our knowledge is limited to that which can be learned from measurement of neural electric pulses.

The cells of the body are enfolded in a membrane that is selectively permeable to the metabolites that are contained inside and outside the cell. Some molecules, such as water (H_2O), pass through without difficulty. A high concentration of glucose molecules outside the cell provides the gradient to force the molecules into the cell, possibly through some "carrier" action in addition to ordinary diffusion processes. The carbon dioxide (CO_2) product of combustion has sufficiently higher concentration inside the cell to diffuse outward. Sodium ions (Na^+) present a special problem, and the difference in sodium-ion concentration is especially important in connection with neural discharges. There is a considerably lower concentration of the sodium ion in the interior (axoplasm) of the nerve cell (approximately 10 mEq/liter* in contrast with a concentration of 142 mEq/liter in the extracellular fluid). Not knowing anything about the real cause, we say that this gradient is maintained

* Milliequivalents per liter.

by means of what is commonly called the "sodium pump." It may be, in fact, that the fluids inside and outside the cell are more semi-crystalline than they are watery. (The polar character of the water molecule, with one side slightly negative in relation to the other side, could presumably bring about the semicrystalline state.) Also, the activity may be much more dynamic, involving oscillatory phenomena of some type.

The potassium concentration inside the cell is approximately thirty-five times its concentration in the extracellular fluid, but potassium ions (K^+) can diffuse through the membrane in either direction with relative freedom. The high concentration of potassium on the inside of the axon is mainly due to the effect of the "sodium pump"; that is, when sodium ions (cations) are moved to the outside of the cell membrane, the reduction of positive ions remaining inside the membrane causes the inside of the cell membrane to become electronegative. The potential difference of the cell interior pulls potassium ions to the interior to compensate for the deficit left by the expelled sodium ions.

By some such process, an electrical potential difference, which constitutes the *membrane potential,* develops between the inside and the outside of the axon. Let us picture a neuron in its normal, non-discharging state, with a potential difference of about 80 millivolts across the axon membrane. Suppose that the axon membrane is electrically stimulated, or disturbed, at some point. The disturbance causes the membrane potential at that point to collapse, probably because that point becomes permeable to sodium ions and the sodium ions rush into the interior of the axon. For an instant, that portion of the membrane becomes positive on the inside and negative (or at least less positive) on the outside. We speak of this as *depolarization* of the membrane, as contrasted with the normal, polarized state. The depolarization propagates in both directions and away from the initial point of disturbance. That is, as more sodium ions flow through the membrane, a *depolarization wave* travels in both directions to the ends of the fiber.

Immediately after a nerve impulse has passed, there is "healing," called *repolarization,* which begins at the same point in the membrane at which depolarization began. The net result of the depolarization wave and of the quick repolarization recovery is that the wave becomes a short electric pulse, called a *nerve impulse, nerve discharge, spike,* or *action potential.* Because the entire process of membrane-potential collapse and restoration can take place so quickly, a neuron can repeat the cycle up to several hundred or a thousand times every second. There is, however, a *stimulus threshold* below which the neuron will not respond. When the neuron does respond, each impulse it transmits will convey approximately the full intensity of its capabilities. This is referred to as the *all-or-nothing* law.

How may one observe the action potential, or spike, of an axon membrane? Mechanical indicators cannot respond quickly enough or with enough sensitivity. Consequently, electrical instruments of

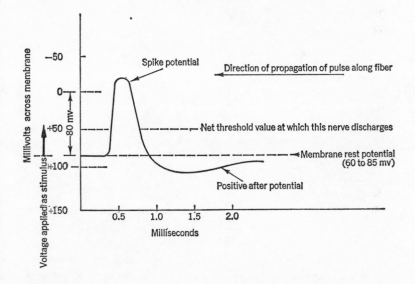

Fig. 13. How a neural pulse (spike) is generated. The potential across the membrane at rest is about 80 mv. When an opposing voltage of about 35 mv (extreme left) is applied to reduce the membrane potential to about 45 mv, sodium ions can surge through the membrane and produce a traveling electric spike of the type shown, the pulse width being about ½ msec. The membrane voltage experiences an overshoot (called positive afterpotential) during recovery. Voltages shown are only approximate, since they vary from nerve to nerve. (From *Introduction to Natural Science.* Courtesy of Academic Press)

the oscilloscope type are used for this purpose. Figure 13 illustrates the form of a single pulse that develops when the nerve fiber is subjected to a single electric stimulus. If the electric stimulus should be repeated rapidly, or if the nerve is continuously subjected to other mechanical or chemical treatment to prolong nerve discharge, there will be repeated discharges until the cause of the discharges is removed. It is from such very similar electric pulses that the nervous system must gather information on the state of the body and of the body's environment and take appropriate action for the proper protection of the body and to control its functioning.

CHAPTER 6

Control Systems of the Body

"Do I contradict myself? Very well, then, I contradict
myself; (I am large. I contain multitudes)."*

Walt Whitman

We must now identify the major neurological control systems that
make possible the beautifully co-ordinated activity of the living
body. The study is likely to elicit new questions as to how this all
came about by evolutionary processes, as well as to set new standards of performance for future electronic computers to match.

Major divisions of the nervous system: the central nervous system

How should one divide and identify a system of neurons that
permeates the entire body from head to toe and that is interconnected in the complex manner described in the previous chapter?
There could be some anatomical arguments for looking separately
at the head, the chest, the arms, and the legs, and the intermediate
regions of the body for its nervous complements. This would not
get us very far, however. The classification of neurons as *receptor*
neurons and *effector* neurons offers a better guide, since many receptor neurons lead from sensory organs located around the periph-
ery of the body to the spine, and effector neurons generally lead
from the spine out to the *peripheral nervous system*. The spinal
column and the brain are difficult to separate into large categories,
and so we call these the *central nervous system*. There is a third
system, called the *autonomic nervous system,* which serves visceral

* *Song of Myself,* from *Leaves of Grass.*

organs, blood vessels, and glands somewhat independently of the other two systems (Fig. 14). In man nearly three quarters of all neuronal cell bodies of the nervous system are located in the *cerebral cortex* of the brain, where one of the principal functions is to store information and memory of experiences. It is in the cortex that the most advanced forms of reasoning, integration of information, and planning of action take place. The most abstract processes of thought and the highest levels of association of information and of concepts take place in the *prefrontal lobe* and in portions of the *temporal* and *parietal lobes*.

Moving from the cerebral cortex downward, we pass through several regions that have functions of distinctly lower level than those of the cortex (Fig. 18). The *hypothalamus* is concerned with the regulation of arterial-pressure and body-fluid balances and with maintenance of secretions of some of the endocrine glands. The sensations of pain and pleasure, anger, wakefulness, alertness, and excitement seem to involve the hypothalamus. Since from personal experience we know that these very sensations also engage the highest level of thought (and therefore the cortex), there must be extensive interconnections that permit the lower centers to command the attention of the cortex whenever there is need to do so. The thalamus also acts to direct the attention of parts of the cortex to specific sensations. The sensation of pain, for example, seems to depend on the thalamus, as does the transmission of the sensations of touch. The interconnecting portion between the cerebral cortex and the spinal column contains large areas of diffuse neurons collectively referred to as the *reticular formation*. Many functions associated with support of the body against the pull of gravity, maintenance of equilibrium, and co-ordinated movements of the body seem to have controls in groups of neurons that are included in the reticular formation. The term *basal ganglia* is also used to designate the large collection of neuronal cells that lie below the cortex and that encompass parts of the thalamus, the hypothalamus, and some lower portions.

In other words, the collections of neuronal cells and fibers that lie in the regions known as the *hypothalamus,* the *thalamus,* the *basal ganglia,* and the *reticular formation* receive sensory impulses that either automatically respond to and act on that sensory information or demand participation on the part of the cortex. We shall note, however, that certain motor functions of the body have connection with the cortex through the *pyramidal system*. Through this, the cortex may direct discrete movements of the fingers, toes, facial muscles, and other motor regions. There is also the *extrapyramidal system*, whereby the brain becomes involved in the control of many parts of the body.

Finally, the central nervous system includes the spinal cord, which consists of large numbers of nerve-cell bodies and nerve fibers that interconnect with the peripheral nerves of the sensory and motor systems. The spinal system has two main lines of connection to the spinal tract, which occur at each vertebra: the *dorsal root* is made up of connections to the sensory organs; the *ventral root* is made up of connections to the motor end organs (Fig. 15).

The neuronal fibers that extend away from the spinal column may go directly to sensory receptors or to motor end organs. However, many of them collect to form neuronal centers from which emanate complex trunks of fibers that lead to various regions of the body. The trunk lines from the *cervical plexus** and the *brachial plexus* lead to the upper regions of the body; those from the *solar plexus* are associated with the upper abdomen; and the *sacral plexus* is concerned with the lower regions of the body.

The autonomic nervous system

The lowest level of the nervous system (lowest in that it involves a minimum of conscious control) is called the *autonomic nervous system*. As shown in Fig. 14 the autonomic nervous system can be subdivided into a *sympathetic,* or *thoracolumbar, division,* which has connections to the thoracic and lumbar regions of the body, and the *parasympathetic,* or *craniosacral, division,* which has its main connections with the cranial and sacral regions. The autonomic system extends efferent nerves directly to the visceral organs such as the heart and the glands and to the muscles that act involuntarily, such as those of the iris. As illustrated in Fig. 14, the neurons join as ganglia outside the spinal cord, many of the ganglia forming longitudinal nerve trunks in the sympathetic system.

While the organs that are directly connected to the autonomic

* A plexus is an interweaving of nerves (from the Latin meaning to *braid*).

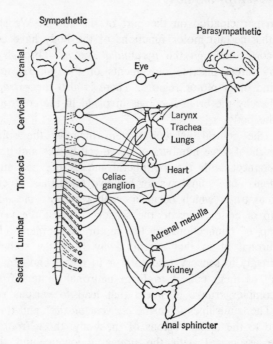

Fig. 14. The autonomic system, illustrating a few of the neural interconnections between the sympathetic and parasympathetic systems and some of the organs of the body.

system perform their functions without need for direct guidance from the brain, their functions can be very much affected by the emotional state of the individual, as each of us knows from personal experience.

The reflex loop, or reflex arc

The third portion of the nervous system is called the *peripheral nervous system*. The afferent-neuron portion of this system leads from the sensory organs, as well as from proprioceptors located in the muscles, joints, and tendons, to the spinal cord and the brain. The efferent, or motoneuron, portion leads from the brain and spinal cord to the muscle system of the body and to certain glands. The muscles that are served include the voluntary (striated) muscles of the hands and feet, but motoneurons also go out to the sweat glands, the salivary glands, the blood vessels, and the heart muscles. The peripheral system therefore represents lines of communication as compared with the more complex role of co-ordination and interpretation, which is exercised by the central nervous system.

Without delving more deeply into the anatomy of the peripheral system we shall find especially interesting the simple reflex function that may involve as little as one afferent and one efferent neuron and a muscle cell to form the *reflex arc,* or *reflex loop.*

For purposes of analysis we take the experience of holding out an arm at full length on initial instructions from the brain. Even with closed eyes we continue to be aware of the position of the arm as we move it. Apparently sensory signals that come from muscle tissues

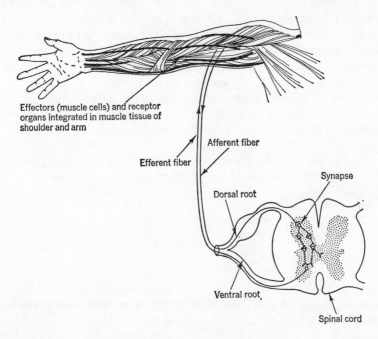

Fig. 15. How the muscle tone, position, and movements are maintained by simple reflex loops. The sensory receptors, which are sensitive to muscle stretch, are so integrated with the muscle tissue as to signal every change in that tissue. The muscle tissue, in turn, automatically adjusts to those signals to maintain its condition. (From *Introduction to Natural Science.* Courtesy of Academic Press)

keep the body informed of the positions and movements of the muscles. If the intention is to hold the arm outward, the signals automatically bring corrective action on the part of the muscles to hold it there. We have, in fact, a *reflex loop* (or *reflex arc*), as illustrated in Fig. 15. This therefore constitutes an *automatic, local control system* whereby individual portions of the muscle and sensory systems maintain equilibrium conditions *with a minimum of involvement on the part of the central nervous system.*

We can understand the importance of these local, automatic control systems even more clearly if we stand in an erect position and attempt to analyze the activities of the various parts of the body. It becomes obvious that to stand erect a vast number of muscle cells comes into play. There is a tendency for the body parts to sway slightly and for the arms and legs to be in slight movement, as if they were hunting for balance points, the very same "hunting" that was discussed in connection with systems that control the temperature of a room or the position of a vehicle. That the control of body muscles is automatic is clear, since all this goes on without conscious mental control of the multitude of local actions. Figure 16 illustrates the control-loop character of the process in terms of control-circuit representation.

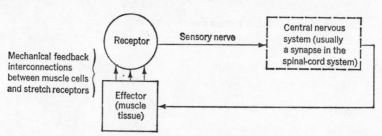

Fig. 16. Representation of the simple reflex control loop involving a stretch receptor that is physically incorporated with effector-muscle tissue.

Effective as these local, automatic reflex actions are, we know that there are many occasions that do require conscious control of muscle action. For example, when the finger feels the sharp point of a pin, we have all the features that are represented by Figs. 15 and 16 plus an additional stimulus that goes from the finger to the conscious areas of the central nervous system (Fig. 17).

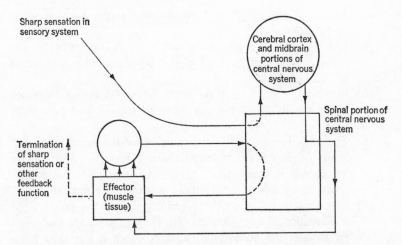

Fig. 17. Example of how a sharp sensation superimposes awareness on the part of the brain, without eliminating the normal simple movements involving sensory neuron-synapse-muscle reflexes. (From *Introduction to Natural Science*. Courtesy of Academic Press)

Nerve connections in muscle

The nerve and muscle activity described above for the reflex arc, or reflex loop, requires a rather intimate relationship of nerve endings in muscle fibers. Receptors include *free nerve endings,* Pacinian corpuscles, and especially *Golgi tendon organs* and *muscle spindles*. In the case of the Golgi tendon organs the nerve fibers that lead to tendons are distributed *throughout* the tendon in such a way that stretch of the tendon causes discharge of the nerves. The discharge therefore occurs regardless of whether the muscle contracts and pulls the tendon, or the muscle is pulled by other means.

End plates that are distributed along muscle fibers connect motoneurons with the muscle. Muscle action requires that a pulse arriving by way of the motoneuron cause activity on the part of a muscle membrane area that is roughly one thousand times the cross-sectional area of the nerve ending as it enters the end plate. This requires a rather large amplification of the energies involved, and it becomes necessary to look for an amplification process to make this possible. The amplification process again involves acetylcholine, with a sequence that seems to be as follows:

(a) Arrival of a pulse at the motoneuron causes release of some acetylcholine.

(b) The acetylcholine diffuses across a small gap between the nerve ending and the end plate and reacts with a receptor in the end plate.

(c) Reaction of the end plate with the acetylcholine increases the permeability of the end plate to sodium and potassium ions.

(d) The end-plate potential is thereby reduced toward zero, and if the original nerve impulse is strong enough, the end-plate membrane is depolarized, causing an impulse to be propagated away from the end plate to excite the muscle.

(e) Immediately following the reaction in (c), the products of the reaction of acetylcholine with the end plate are destroyed by the enzyme acetylcholinesterase, which is normally present at the end plates.

Inhibitory functions of the nervous system

The reflex reactions involving sensory-nerve impulses and motor functions also include *restraining,* or *inhibitory, action* of nerve impulses so that the contraction and relaxation of co-operating muscles is smooth and co-ordinated. The ability to play an instrument such as a piano or an organ or to participate in a sport such as tennis or basketball shows how successful the co-ordination of the sensory system with the motor system can be. In this way many daily experiences, including many of the intrinsic life processes of the body, are either fully controlled by the spinal cord or controlled co-operatively by it, with only moderate involvement of the subcortical and cortical regions of the brain.

The fundamental principles of cybernetics are beautifully illustrated by the motor system of the body. The system is organized into two anatomically separated portions at the level of the medulla, with two sets of spinal connections (Fig. 18). Because of its anatomical structure, one of these is called the *pyramidal system* and actually consists of a tract called the *corticospinal tract.* The left side of Fig. 18 lists the muscle systems that are controlled directly by the corresponding listed portions of the cortex.

The *extrapyramidal system* is composed of several additional

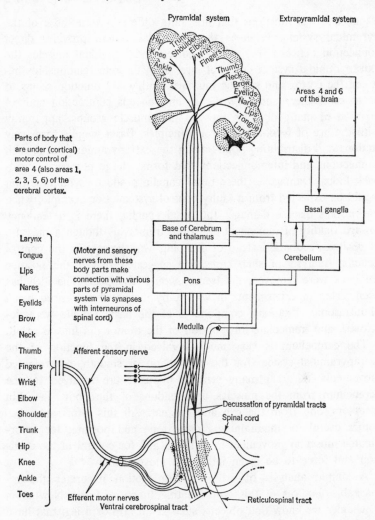

Fig. 18. A generalized scheme representing the motor controls exercised by the pyramidal (corticospinal) system and the extrapyramidal (extra-corticospinal) system. The latter, shown at the right, consists largely of interconnections between the various parts of the central nervous system that contribute toward precise motor control of the muscle system. Note that the pathways are illustrated for one side only. (From *Introduction to Natural Science.* Courtesy of Academic Press)

tracts, and has functions that are quite different from those of the pyramidal system. Whereas the pyramidal system provides direct connection between the cerebral cortex and individual muscles the extrapyramidal system does not have such discrete relationships between the cortex and specific muscles. Rather, its function seems to be to *co-ordinate* and *control* the simultaneous contraction and relaxation of many different muscles and muscle groups, apparently with the use of feedback control principles. Basal ganglia form way stations and distributing points along the extrapyramidal tracts, with connections and interconnections that form a large number of feedback loops. Damage to these basal ganglia produces symptoms that would be expected from a faulty control system. For example, when Parkinson's disease damages the basal ganglia, there is a tendency toward rigidity of movement and even tremor, as though a measure of positive feedback instead of damping were present in the control system. Analysis of such cases has suggested that if the positive feedback were removed, the tremor would disappear. The idea has been tested in experiments in which, by means of a focused beam of ultrasonic vibrations, components of the basal ganglia were destroyed, and immediate interruption of the tremor did indeed result.

The cerebellum is very much involved in the function of the extrapyramidal system for the production of smooth, co-ordinated movements. A great many sensory impulses are received by the cerebellum from the muscles and tendons of the body, the skin receptors, and from the eye and the ear. All this information becomes useful for maintaining muscle tone and posture, for co-ordinated muscular movement in walking, and for control of the duration and force to be given individual movements.

A simple analysis of arm and leg motion illustrates the remarkable features of this co-ordinating function. From Newtonian mechanics we know that objects, such as an arm or a leg, that have inertia require a force to give them motion, and that, once started, still other forces are required to bring them to a stop. How is it that a normal individual can move his foot rapidly, then stop it automatically at a selected position without overshoot and without any apparent help from the cerebral cortex? Judging from all electromechanical experiences, unless some elaborate control devices are incorporated in the system the momentum of the leg would carry the foot *beyond* the desired point, and the eyes and proprioceptor mechanisms would have to initiate movement to bring the foot back to the projected point. In fact, only after several such movements would the foot finally reach the desired point. Fortunately there are incorporated within the experience and "memory" of the extrapyramidal system (more especially the cerebellum) the means whereby, even before the leg reaches its destination, there come into play "feedback" impulses that apply appropriate "braking" contractions of opposing muscles (or inhibitory impulses) to slow up and stop the motion at the proper point. In this way the foot can be brought to rest at a desired position without overshoot. The prevention of overshoot by the cerebellum is called the *damping* function of the cerebellum and is illustrated in schematic form in Fig. 19. Damage to the cerebellum can cause exactly the overshoot conditions that have just been described.

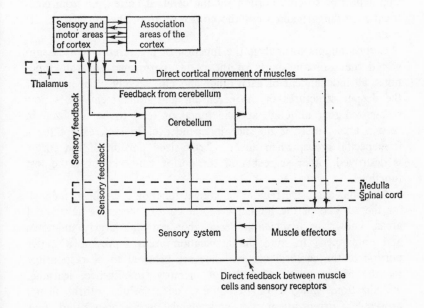

Fig. 19. Schematic of motor (muscle) control system illustrating the role of the cerebellum. (From *Introduction to Natural Science.* Courtesy of Academic Press)

The cerebral cortex

Although the cerebral cortex may participate in reflex functions, its capabilities extend far beyond simple reflex responses. The decisions, or "feedback," it produces for dealing with a situation are likely to be the "output" of long years of education preparation and many years of experience. Like the memory attributed to elephants, the time lapse between an event that initiates feedback and its actual appearance may be the whole lifetime of a person. The method of applying the feedback may involve very carefully planned steps or a program of steps. As an example, we refer to the psychiatrist who tries to reveal the relationship of childhood experiences with later behavior in adulthood.

It is ironic that of all the parts of the nervous system the least understood is the cerebral cortex. Such information as we do have has been obtained from observation of the effects of destruction or stimulation of specific portions of the cerebral cortex, or from electrical recordings taken from the cortex or from the surface of the scalp.

Early attempts to analyze the function of the cerebral cortex suggested that different parts of the cortex performed separate functions, all independent of each other and also largely independent of the deeper structures of the cerebrum and brain stem. It is now recognized that although specific functions tend to be localized in certain areas, there is no such independence. In fact, except for a few specific areas, when any moderate-sized portion of the cortex is destroyed, other segments of the cortex can take over the lost functions.

Although extensive regions of known function have been mapped for the surface of the human cerebral cortex, there are substantial areas, known as *association areas,* that are still largely unknown and unmapped. In man the association areas represent a major portion of the cerebral cortex. They are believed to be responsible for the highly advanced traits of memory, intelligence, learning, verbalization, imagination, emotions, and various other mental processes. Current attempts to understand how the association areas function and to explain intellectual and mental processes in terms of neuronal behavior have only given rise to limited evidence and speculation.

The feedback theory of sleep and wakefulness

There are some neurophysiologists who contend that the highest levels of integration and mental processes do not reside solely in the neurons of the cerebral cortex. They propose instead that these functions are significantly aided by a region extending through the central portion of the brain stem called the *reticular formation,* or *reticular system.* According to this hypothesis the reticular system is primarily concerned with arousing the cerebral cortex to receive and interpret incoming sensory signals, and to contribute to the regulation of all motor activities of the body as well. In this particular respect some authors compare the reticular system to a traffic-control center that helps to direct the flow of messages to the brain and alerts the conscious centers to activity.

One of the interesting puzzles involving cerebral function concerns the diurnal cycle of sleep and wakefulness. Research indicates that even when a person remains in total darkness or in total light, he continues to maintain approximately the same sleep/wakefulness cycle, within a period of about twenty-four hours. Evidence also indicates that the mechanisms controlling sleeping and waking are intimately related to those that involve emotion and attention. *148389*

Between the darkness out of which individuals are born and the ultimate darkness that is death, there is a daily ebb and flow of light to which each of us irresistibly submits. It is estimated that a third of life is spent in sleep. Why all this sleep? Why must an individual plunge into periods of stillness?

Electrical studies of the brain show that when an individual is awake, many nerve impulses pass continuously through the nervous system, never ceasing. When an individual is asleep, however, only a limited number of neuronal discharges continue. Consequently the state of wakefulness appears to represent a high degree of activity on the part of the cerebrum, while the state of sleep represents a much lower degree of activity. The explanations are inconclusive.

Stimulation of the reticular activating system causes nerve impulses to spread upward and eventually to excite the cortex. However, the reticular activating system itself must be stimulated to action by input signals from other sources. When an animal such as a cat is asleep, the reticular activating system is in an almost totally dormant state, yet almost any type of sensory signal can immediately activate the system. For example, pain stimuli from any part of the body, or proprioceptor signals from the joints or muscles, impulses from the cortex, or a loud auditory stimulus (the buzz of an electric alarm) can all cause immediate activation of the reticular activating system. This is called the *arousal reaction,* and it is the means by which sensory stimuli awaken people from deep sleep.

As activation of the reticular system arouses the cerebral cortex, the latter further increases the activity of the reticular system. It would seem that the interrelationship between the reticular system and the cortex represents *positive* feedback up to the state of full wakefulness or down to the state of deep sleep; that is, the states of full wakefulness and deep sleep represent terminal states, and transition from one state to the other is usually accomplished by progressive stages in which positive-feedback interrelationships play a role. The feedback is assumed to be positive because negative feedback would tend to hold the system in its existing state.

The reticular formation may also be involved in another "feedback loop," which sends impulses down the spinal cord to increase body muscle tone that in turn excites muscle proprioceptors to send sensory impulses upward to excite the brain system. Finally, a third form of feedback involves stimulation of the *sympathetic nerves* by the reticular formation. This causes the release of epinephrine (adrenalin) by the adrenal gland, which powerfully enhances the activity of the reticular system, particularly in the region associated with autonomic responses involving fear or anger.

Thus it seems possible to formulate a theory on wakefulness and sleep based on the existence of three feedback loops within the reticular formation—the cerebral cortex, the body muscles, and the adrenal gland via the hormone epinephrine. It is conjectured that after prolonged wakefulness many of the neuronal cells of the feedback loops become fatigued or become less active for other reasons. When this happens, feedback produces further depression of the reticular activating system until the state of sleep is achieved.

Can an individual have various degrees of wakefulness and sleep? The answer lies in the realization that the feedback loops contain literally millions of parallel pathways. If the feedback system is operating through only a few of these, an individual is only slightly awake, but if the feedback is operating through large numbers of pathways simultaneously, he is wide awake.

Evidence in favor of the feedback theory of sleep and wakefulness is the finding that complete relaxation of the muscles throughout the body can frequently cause a person to go to sleep even in the absence of muscular or neuronal fatigue.*

There are two distinct phases of sleep: One is accompanied by *rapid eye movements* and is called *REM sleep.* The other is *non-rapid-eye-movement,* or *NREM, sleep.* The periods of REM sleep are short early in the night and lengthen toward morning, with an average length of twenty minutes. Approximately fifty to seventy minutes after onset of sleep, the initial REM period of the night begins. The periods recur every eighty to ninety minutes and constitute 20–25% of the conventional night's sleep of young adults.

It is believed that dreaming sleep and REM sleep are identical. During the dream period there is scanning of visual events, along with other physiological manifestations such as increased respiration, heart rate, gastric secretion, and adrenal corticoid secretion. It appears that the brain is highly active during REM sleep and seems to be "perceiving" and "reacting" to its percepts much as the awake brain does. The function of REM sleep is currently under investigation.

* Kleitman, N., *Sleep and Wakefulness* (Chicago: Univ. of Chicago Press, 1963).

CHAPTER 7

Neural Processes and Computers

"It is dangerous to identify the real physical (or biological) world with the models which are constructed to explain it. The problem of understanding the animal nervous action is far deeper than the problem of understanding the mechanism of a computing machine. Even plausible explanations of nervous reaction should be taken with a very large grain of salt."

John Von Neumann

For many cyberneticists an introduction to brain function leads fairly directly toward comparisons with computer models and computers. However, we have yet to probe the nature of the neural pulses and the processes whereby they are "coded" and transformed into appropriate motor pulses to direct body activity. The processes presented thus far apply to simple as well as to complex animal organisms. Before long we shall make transition to a realm of phenomena that as far as we can tell is reserved to man alone. Included in this are the phenomena of language,* conceptual and symbolic thinking, and capability for analysis of processes, which are identified under the general title of *information theory*. We shall note some interesting parallels between the brain and the networks of computers when exploring elements of information theory. The parallels are more superficial than real, however, as one tries to identify computer and brain function with the long and complex reaches of memory, emotion, passion, and creativity.

---

* This is not to dispute that some other animals can communicate with each other.

Coding of neural data

We noted that receptor neurons and effector neurons communicate with each other through synaptic regions. In the case of input signals that engage the brain, one may think of the entire spinal cord and brain as constituting a synaptic region that provides billions of interconnected neurons serving the purposes of the body.

Before proceeding with the question of how neuronal pulses are interpreted, we require a few more details on the pulses themselves. For example, how do the signals generated by the visual organs compare with those received from other sensory systems? How do the signals received from a particular organ vary with intensity or frequency or type of stimulus on that organ? In other words, what are the "raw data" available to the brain from which the brain must derive meaning through some coding process?

We noted that when a receptor sensory organ is sufficiently sensitized (at or above the threshold value), an electric pulse called *spike potential* is generated and caused to travel along the axon to a synapse. Unlike the contacting of an electric switch, the neuron quickly recovers and is ready to generate another pulse if the irritation persists. Its recovery period, called *refractory period,* during which it cannot "fire," is substantially shorter if it continues to be subject to a strong stimulus. This variation in rate of firing can therefore be useful to the brain for judging the nature and intensity of the stimulus.

The characteristics of neural discharges that permit the brain to distinguish one stimulus and "information" from another are the following:

(a) *Frequency of Pulses.* There is, we observed, an increase in the number of pulses that a single neuron discharges when the stimulus persists. There is also an increase in frequency received by the CNS when the stimulus is sufficiently intense to stimulate more neurons. It seems clear, therefore, that *intensity of stimuli* can be distinguished by what amounts to a system of *frequency modulation,** or frequency variation. Intensities can also be compared,

---

* Frequency modulation is very useful for radio transmission and for other transmission of signals to reduce the effects of background noise and of fluctuations in amplification. For that purpose the circuit is designed to convert changes in the variable (temperature, voltage, sound intensity, etc.) to changes

either directly when signals are concurrent, or, less successfully, by use of memory.

(b) *Spatial or Organ Discrimination.* With the exception of pain sensations there is little difficulty in identifying the receptor organ or the part of the body from which signals come. There is little difficulty, for example, in distinguishing between sight and hearing, or the effects of sitting on a sharp needle versus sitting on a comfortable chair that provides a substantial seating area.

(c) *Time-Rate Aspect.* The timing or frequency of neural impulses offers additional information on the nature of a stimulus. For example, the pattern of frequencies coming from the ear will tell all that needs to be known about the frequency and intensity of a note as well as the beginning and end of the piece of music. Or the changes in over-all intensity, plus the local pitch variations that come with changing distance and speed from a source of sound, tell whether one is approaching or going away from the source of the sound.

The effect of change is further illustrated by holding a comb against the hand. The over-all size of the comb, the number of its teeth, and the pressure on the hand can all be distinguished. If the comb is also pulled along the hand, the sensory organs will now convey additional information on the nature of the stimulus.

(d) *Combination of Sensory Data.* As has been noted earlier, concurrent impulses coming from different sensory organs combine to give additional significance to the neural impulses received from any one organ. Even when listening to music, the scope of appreciation is greatly increased when we can also see the orchestra and feel the reverberations in the room.

(e) *Influence of Experience and of Memory.* Finally it seems that every neural experience is likely to gain or lose informational value, depending on the experiences of earlier days that have become established as part of memory.

These, then, seem to be the "raw material" of neural discharges and patterns out of which the central nervous system must com-

in the frequency of the transmitted pulse. This conversion represents a form of coding, so decoding is necessary at the receiver end of the circuit.

pose an understanding of the quality, the modality, the intensity, and the significance of the stimulus to which the body is being subjected at any instant.

Synaptic influences on neuronal discharges

In the same way, let us list the effects that a signal from an afferent nerve may experience when it enters a synapse:

(a) The signals that arrive from the peripheral nervous system or the internal organs of the body tend to have the nature of *discrete electric pulses,* or spikes, that are characteristic of the particular receptor neuron and of the intensity conditions of the stimulus causing the neural discharges.

(b) On entering the synapse, the axons of the neurons tend to branch into telodendria. The *spike energies become divided* in a complex way and produce electric pulses or chemical products that are graduated instead of remaining discrete.

(c) The synapse provides vast numbers of interneurons that interconnect each neuron with many other neurons and cause many neurons to converge on one or a few neurons. (This may be thought of as a process of *addition* or *multiplication.*)

(d) The interneurons and interconnections bring into play neurons that serve the function of *inhibiting* the action of certain neurons. (This may be thought of as a form of *subtraction* or *division.*)

(e) Because the synaptic interconnections are so extensive and also include the brain, extensive *feedback* influences are made possible. The feedback may be the result of only a few interconnections within the synapse; or it may be the product of the brain or of memory associated with the brain imposing an influence from past neural experiences.

Excursion into computer concepts

Electronic computers are frequently compared with the human brain, often with the implications that some computers are well on the way toward surpassing the human brain not only with respect to computing ability but also with respect to thinking and reasoning. Now that we have some inkling of the nature of the neural messages that supply the brain, it will be useful to attempt a brief excursion into the comparable elements that relate to computer technology. Our purpose in this excursion is simply to identify some similarities and differences, not to answer the question whether man is being threatened by the machine.

In contrast with most machines of the Industrial Revolution, the value of computers is judged not on the basis of the large quantities of energy that they put to use but by the number and types of computing functions they can perform. Usually their performance is compared with the performance of humans. A large computer can, in a matter of minutes and at a cost of a few dollars, equal the output of thousands of hours of human effort. (Of course, there has to be a sufficient load on such an expensive machine to reduce the hourly costs to small amounts.)

The elements that make such machines useful for ordinary arithmetic manipulations are easily understood. We have all become expert in transforming the abstract numbers 1, 2, 3, etc., into material quantities to which we may apply the terms apples, pears, amperes, inches, degrees of rotation, pulses, relay operations, etc. The abstract concept 2+2=4 finds its easy counterpart in two apples plus two apples equal four apples; a two-inch length taken ten times gives the product of twenty inches, and a relay closing and punching paper eight times can represent some event having occurred eight times. Subtraction and division are as easily performed. Since all computations are made up of combinations of these four manipulations, it is easy to understand why computers are so useful. A great many kinds of mechanical and electromechanical devices have been developed for computational purposes based on these simple concepts, and we shall not attempt to categorize them. There is one distinction among them that it is important to make for our purposes, however. The distinction has to do with whether they are of the *analogue* or the *digital* type.

Analogue computers take advantage of any of a wide variety of quantities that are continuously variable and that have linear properties. The flow of time is such a quantity. A wheel or gear can be made to rotate smoothly in almost infinitesimal steps, and the amount of its rotation can be made to bear a linear relationship to number, or time, or length, or number of bushels of wheat processed, or the direction of a ship at sea. When that same wheel is incorporated in a special kind of electric motor called a *servomotor* and connected properly to a second servomotor, the second motor can be made to follow the turns that are given to the first motor. These together constitute a *servomechanism system*.

The odometer/speedometer that translates wheel rotation of an automobile into meter readings in miles or miles-per-hour is an analogue device. The electric meter that reads in amperes and the mechanical gauge that reads in millimeters have the elements of analogue computers, for in each case a measure or feature is produced that is *analogous,* or related in some way, to a physical situation or a physical change. The amplifier that reproduces music or speech from a microphone or phonograph record is an analogue device because there is a *built-in, designed relationship* of sound to the movement of the microphone diaphragm and of the phonograph needle. The use of analogue-computer principles is very wide indeed, including also measurement of body functions such as heartbeat rate as function of exercise, weight as function of diet conditions, or blood-cell count as function of intake of medicine. However, in most applications of these principles the precision or accuracy of devices is dependent on the accuracy with which mechanical parts are machined or the electrical features are calibrated. These weaknesses are not as severe in the second large category, namely the digital computers, to which we shall turn after a brief introduction to the binary notation for writing numbers.

Binary notation

In contrast with the demand for continuous variability and accuracy of construction and function on the part of analogue computers, digital computers call only for a capacity to identify clearly the condition "on" or "off" of any constituent electrical or mechanical element. We can demonstrate the principle simply by turning on an ordinary light switch in a room; the light goes on when we turn the switch to the ON position, and it goes off when we turn the switch to the OFF position. It makes no difference if we use a mercury switch, a toggle switch, or a rotary switch; nor does it matter whether the light that goes on and off is of 25-, 50-, or 100-watt capacity. The significance of the act lies in the ON versus OFF position. Nor are we limited to electric circuits, for a relay going on or off is just as significant, especially if it is set up to make a noise, or punch paper tape, or cause spots to become magnetized on a magnetic tape. For example, if the electric spike potentials that travel down the axon of a neuron were amplified sufficiently to operate a relay, we could punch holes on a moving paper roll to give a visible record of the number of spikes that the nerve discharges.

This, however, does not answer the question of what makes an on-off device so useful as a computer. For that we must recognize a few other conditions as well—namely, that an "on" condition of an electric circuit or mechanical device can represent the digit 1. Alternatively, the circuit going off could be said to represent the digit 0. We then have a two-digit representation for on-off.

Even this identification would carry little meaning, however, were it not for the fact that the two positions (or two symbols) represented by on-off (or by 1-0) can be used to represent any other number, large or small, if we resort to the use of the binary system for writing numbers. Ordinarily we employ the decimal system, which uses the numbers 0, 1, 2, 3, 4, 5, 6, 7, 8, and 9. With these we begin with a decimal point and let the first number to the left of the decimal point represent units, the next to the left represent ten times the unit, the next to the left one hundred times, etc. Moving to the right of the decimal point divides the units by ten, then by one hundred, etc. A number such as 128.53 then represents $8 \times 1 + 2 \times 10 + 1 \times 100 + 5 \times \frac{1}{10} + 3 \times \frac{1}{100}$. But the decimal system, with its base of ten, is only one of many possible systems. We can also use the base two for writing numbers, which gives the *binary system*. In binary notation each next position to the left corresponds to a multiplication by two instead of by the ten of the decimal system. The first position represents $2^0 = 1$ (that is, two raised to the zero power equals one). The next position to the left represents $2^1 = 2$, the next to the left $2^2 = 4$, etc. The basic array would then represent $2^6 \times 2^5 \times 2^4 \times 2^3 \times 2^2 \times 2^1 \times 2^0$ (instead of $10^6 \times 10^5 \times 10^4 \times 10^3 \times 10^2 \times 10^1 \times 10^0$ of the decimal system) with respect to the *positions* of the numbers. We can tabulate these powers of two as follows, recalling that $2^6 = 2 \times 2 \times 2 \times 2 \times 2 \times 2 = 64$, $2^3 = 2 \times 2 \times 2 = 8$, etc., and writing the actual value below the power:

2^6	2^5	2^4	2^3	2^2	2^1	2^0
64	32	16	8	4	2	1

Thus the seventh position to the left ($=2^6$) represents the value 64. The fourth position to the left ($=2^3$) has the value 8, etc. Of course in the decimal system, for each position we must insert one of the digits from 0 to 9. In the binary system, however, since we use only one of two values (namely 0 or 1, corresponding to the "off" or the "on" position, respectively), all that is required to register the value corresponding to that position is a relay being on or off. Therefore the number 5 would be written in the binary system as 101, because this would represent $1 \times 2^2 + 0 \times 2^1 + 1 \times 2^0 = 4 + 0 + 1 = 5$. The number 8 would be written as 1000 (representing $1 \times 2^3 + 0 \times 2^2 + 0 \times 2^1 + 0 \times 2^0 = 8 + 0 + 0 + 0$). And it is all done by relays going on or off at each digit position.

We note that the binary system is in a sense quite prodigal in its use of digits and might therefore be considered to be inefficient. For example, the term 1000000 in the binary system represents only a value of 64 in the decimal system. Indeed many more digits have to be used than are required in the decimal notation. Correspondingly, each of the ten digits of the decimal system conveys more information than is encompassed in the 1 or the 0 of the binary notation. Nevertheless, because the binary notation requires only the "on" or "off" selection, it lends itself more easily to computer use.

Of course the value of knowing whether a switch is on or off lies in the information that that knowledge represents. How much information content is there in knowing the answer to an "either-or" question? It turns out that according to information theory (which we cannot delve into in any detail) the informational content of a two-step operation such as "on-off" is given by the logarithm of two to the binary base two, which equals unity; that is, information content $= \log_2 2 = 1$. This information is called a *bit,* which is a contraction of "binary unit." Each bit therefore represents the knowledge that a circuit is either on or off.* We shall now turn to some examples of its use as elements in digital computers.

Digital computers

Suppose we have the value 64, which is to be written in binary notation as 1000000. How would a computer (or a mechanical typewriter) "write" this? The operation is simple. In moving from position to position, the machine would pass over each position that had 0, but wherever there appeared the number 1, the machine could

---

* In contrast, the decimal system represents informational content equivalent to $\log_2 10 = 3.32$ bits, since selection of any one of its ten digits conveys considerably more meaning than does the identification of "on" versus "off."

punch a card (or magnetize a spot on a magnetic tape). The significance of the record would then lie only in whether there is a punched hole (or magnetized spot) *at each position* of the card (or tape). The accuracy of the record lies only in the *position* being correct and in the punched hole (or magnetized spot) being clearly detectable.

But now that we have a record in binary notation, what do we do with it? For its use in computation we must inquire how one may add and subtract with such a system. Let us see what significance can be given to a system that depends only on being able to distinguish "on" from "off," to which to relate the digits 1 and 0, respectively. We might apply these principles to the evaluation data that are collected by the census bureau, where each questionnaire provides small circles that can be darkened and later "read" by electronic scanners. Every time the scanner sees a darkened circle it might operate something corresponding to a relay. Some circles are simply added up. Many other combinations are possible, however. For example, one particular "relay" might be designed to operate only when three specific circles are all darkened on a questionnaire. The principles and techniques apply in the same way if one is utilizing computers for control of inventory for a national distributor. In any case, as the "relays" operate in one combination or another, other mechanisms would register the results on tape or on cards or type out the results on other paper.

Indeed the electronic computer can take the raw data collected from such tabulations and perform a wide range of functions to obtain the results that are desired. Circuits can be included that perform either positive or negative (inhibitory) functions when the switch is on. A computer can also be coded so that the punched holes in specific portions of a card system will "tell" the computer what kind of function to perform on that card—multiplication, subtraction, or whatever. The data from cards can be stored in coded form in the memory bank of the computer's magnetic tape. Each item of coded memory can have its own location or "address," and a card can direct the computer to utilize the coded instruction or data that are at that address; that is, a series of punched spaces in a particular spot on a card or tape need not designate only the digits 1 and 0. The series can, instead, be a code that says, "Divide the number now on the computer register by the number found in memory bank station numbered 36."

The operations indicated above appear somewhat cumbersome, and indeed they would be were it not for two virtues that are possessed by electronic computers. The first is the speed with which such computers can check and act on the presence or absence of punched holes or magnetized spots. (The time interval required to recognize the code on a card or tape and to initiate the action required is measured in microseconds.) The second virtue of electronic computers is the speed with which a series of steps can be repeated. This allows the computer to perform additions or subtractions in steps, repeating each step rapidly until the computation with the particular numbers involved is complete. The high speed is exceedingly important for attacking difficult problems, especially when the computation requires a series of approximations until there is clearer evaluation of the problem; that is, the first operation may offer only a rough approximation to a solution, and repeated operations are required to give better and better approximations until the task is complete. The process is then said to be *iterative,* and the ability to undertake iterative approximations rapidly is one of the features that give electronic digital computers their great value. The iterative process also represents a form of feedback, in that the results of every operation, every approximation, become incorporated and utilized in succeeding operations. There is also the virtue that each recognition of the existence of an "on" or an "off" condition at each coded portion of a card or tape can be accomplished with a minimum of error.

This all-too-brief introduction to the principles of digital computers scarcely does justice to the new performance capabilities that are being realized from the application of computers to almost every field of human endeavor.

Comparison of neuronal activity with computers

The neurons of the nervous system may be considered to be equivalent to a diode, or transistor, in a digital computer.* Each may be viewed as an indicator or source of information as to

---

* The electric diode passes current in only one direction and can be made to pass or not pass a current. The newest computers have progressed to integrated circuit elements, which in a sense may be closer to the functional features of the synapse.

whether a circuit is on or off, where a spike in the neuron axon would represent the circuit "on" condition. Both the nervous system and electronic systems utilize electrical pulses. In the case of the nervous system there are also such accompaniments as conversion from light, heat, touch, taste, or smell into electric pulses and reconversion of at least some of this electric energy into chemical changes and muscle activity. Computers also utilize conversions such as mechanical or chemical or magnetic changes into electric pulses and sometimes back again to magnetic or mechanical functions. Both have extensive interconnections among the neuronal units, transistors, and related circuits. Both have memory banks from which to recall and to utilize the experiences of the past. Both depend on "bits" of information as input. Both have built-in logic procedures with which to process the information input. Both can undertake computation that either follows a direct procedure or that utilizes iterative approximations toward final solutions.

But while these similarities are impressive, the differences are equally impressive. An electronic computer may have many thousands of diodes and transistors, but these scarcely compare with the billions of neurons or the tens of billions of interconnections that exist in the human body. An electronic transistor is physically quite small (of the order of millimeters), but this is still nearly a million times larger than the cell body of a neuron. Each tiny transistor requires about $\frac{1}{10}$–$\frac{1}{5}$ watt to operate, against energies that are less in the neuron by factors of 100,000–1,000,000. Because of the small size of neurons, it is possible to provide memory storage in the brain for something like 10^{13}–10^{15} bits of information, which is about a million million times larger than is provided for in the memory banks of even large computers. With all this enormously greater complexity and flexibility, the human brain still weighs only about one pound, against the weight of many tons for the larger computers.

The human brain therefore enjoys a complexity, and with it a degree of flexibility, that far surpasses that of any computer system yet in being or in plan. It is this flexibility that permits the brain to be adaptive to the needs of both common and unusual situations. The complexity and flexibility also seem to be required for creativeness and for abstract thought. However, it is this same flexibility that makes the brain less suited for performing precisely programmed functions. The brain tires of sameness even when it is capable of repeating identical operations over and over again. The computer, on the other hand, never tires of performing the routine functions that are designed into it and required of it, and of doing this with a speed that is many orders of magnitude greater than can be expected of the brain.

Before leaving this comparison, we might ask if the neurological system is more like an analogue computer or a digital computer? We recall that in an analogue computer the basic elements require that there be an output that has some graded or proportional relationship to the input, such as the weight in pounds corresponding to the numbers on the scale of a weighing machine. Digital computers, on the other hand, simply identify the "on" versus the "off" condition in the input from which to derive information and a final answer. The fact that the spikes generated in neural axons are fairly uniform in amplitude and that the *number* of spikes propagated per second increases with stimulus intensity suggests that the brain utilizes binary notation and a digital system for processing information. This is not altogether true, however, for several reasons.

To begin with, there are some differences in spike amplitude and form with changing intensity of stimulus, which means that the brain must utilize some of the proportionality principles of analogue computers to identify stimuli. Moreover, as we observed in the discussion of transmission of signals through synapses, the uniform character of spikes breaks down completely when the energy of a spike becomes distributed unequally among the telodendria and when chemical and electrical effects develop that are the result of many mutually supporting and inhibitory effects. The brain therefore utilizes principles that are characteristic of both analogue computers and digital computers. Of course there is the possibility that the brain utilizes other principles as well that our relatively crude measuring devices have not yet revealed to us.

Relationship to information theory*

The discussions of neural processes to this point are probably adequate for the purposes of most readers. There is some value never-

---

* The paperbacks by Crosson and Sayre and by Singh, in References, make excellent companion books for more details on many of the topics introduced in the remainder of this chapter. The former contains excellent footnotes and bibliographic references on the general implications of information theory.

theless in exploring some of the early ideas on neural processes and neural networks, especially since these were the forerunners of the science of cybernetics. The subject continues to draw interest on the part of research scientists who are probing the details of the processes whereby the brain transforms neural pulses into meaningful information, intelligence, and suitable body activity.

Within the past few decades there has been some effort to view neural phenomena from the more general point of view of the role of communication processes in human affairs. Speech, language, writing, and printing techniques developed slowly to complement and extend the more primitive uses of sounds and signs that were part of the natural endowment of animal life. These not only enormously increased the possibilities for communication, they also provided for the continuous development of language and communication techniques to meet the evolutionary changes of man's society.

Invention of telegraphic and telephonic and later of wireless and television devices added considerably to the technical possibilities. Even these added capabilities did not quite satisfy society's desire for faster (if not more meaningful and truthful) communication. The propaganda mills of social groups, industrial groups, political parties, and national and international agencies demanded ever more and faster communication channels. As telegraph lines and radio and television channels became crowded, there was need to examine the question of the ultimate capabilities of electrical channels for transmitting information. How many broadcast channels could be accommodated within the frequency ranges that were available for radio and television broadcasting? Within each channel, what was the optimum frequency range that permitted communication of intelligence without excessive interference between channels? Which broadcasting techniques permitted faithful reproduction at the listener's end of information that was fed in from the speaker's end? How could the interference due to static (such as interference from neighboring electric lines, electric storms, fluctuations in atmospheric conditions, fluctuations in electron movements, etc.) be reduced?

These and other considerations eventually led to analysis of each element that enters into a communications system from the point of view of ultimate capability, efficiency, and cost for communicating information. At the input end there is the question of the capabilities of language itself and of the informational value inherent in the letters, idioms, and words of the language or code for purposes of communication through electric media.

What constitutes information? There is informational value in the number symbols 1, 2, 3, etc. Also in the letters a, b, c, . . . of the alphabet. Ordinarily the informational significance of each number or letter does not lie in its shape or color or design. Rather, it lies in its relationship to the series of numbers or the letters of the alphabet, respectively. Therefore, selecting the letter k represents a selection of that particular letter from a sequence of twenty-six letters, whereas if we deal with a binary, or on-off, sequence the choice becomes limited to one of only two alternatives. The informational or novelty value of the selection from an on-off sequence therefore is very limited compared to the significance (or novelty) of selecting the letter k from a sequence of twenty-six.

For example, if a mother hears one of her two children coming into the house it is easy to guess whether it is Johnny or Mary. The probability would be 50% that it is the one or the other. If there were many more children in the family, however, she would have difficulty in guessing which of them might be tramping into the house, since there are many more alternatives, and the probabilities for guessing the right individual would be greatly reduced. In a sense, therefore, the informational value of any piece of news is related in some way to its novelty or improbability, or with the likelihood (or probability) of being able to guess that piece of news. That is, there is little informational content or novelty in guessing the presence of someone who is usually hanging around anyway.

With these general ideas in mind, and with the interests of a communications engineer, C. E. Shannon proposed an important theory on the informational content that one can assign to a source of many messages. The informational value of each message is given by the product of the probability of that message being sent times the logarithm of that same probability. On this basis an "alphabet" comprising only two digits (such as "on" and "off") has the informational value of only one "bit." The full English alphabet of twenty-six letters plus a space, on the other hand, permits much greater variety and novelty, so that on the assumption (incorrect) that the letters all have the same probability of being used, the informational value of each letter becomes 4.7 bits. Of course the actual informational content of the English alphabet becomes reduced when one takes into account the rules of language, which limit the occurrence of certain letters. For example, the fact that the letter u always follows the letter q detracts from their informational value as a pair. The fact that the letter x may never follow any of several other letters detracts from its usefulness. On the other hand, these same rules and restrictions on a language make it easier to detect errors, as when the letter x occurs where s is expected. These syntactical rules do introduce constraints on the use of language, to which the term *redundancy* is often applied. The same constraints add greatly to the understanding of speech, especially when the presence of "noise" interferes with clear transmission or when poor enunciation requires that one must guess at some of what is being said. The end effect of all these influences is to assign a value nearer 1 bit per symbol for the English language.

At any rate, the capabilities of the language (or signs, or key operation in the case of the Morse telegraphic code) that constitute *input* to a communications system can be analyzed in such terms. An analysis can also be made of the capabilities and problems of the electrical channels and networks through which the message is coded and sent. Then, finally, the signal must be decoded and received by the one for whom the message is intended. All these constitute elements of a communications system, and the guidelines for making an analysis of the total system are often given the general title of *information theory*. We shall return to this theme in chapter 10 in connection with the entropy concept.

"Thinking" machines and neural networks

We have seen that codes such as binary notation are capable of reducing numbers, letters of the alphabet, and even instructions to symbols that consist of a series of two signs, representing the "off" and the "on" condition. A message made up of such symbols and simple markings can then be "written," or punched, or given magnetic representation, on cards or on magnetic tapes. When fed into a digital computer that is capable of "reading" and responding to the simple symbols and instructions, such cards or tapes can direct the machine to make computations or to perform any other act that has been designed into its electromechanical capabilities.

Even before digital computers had advanced to their present complex forms, there were those who wondered to what extent machines

could be turned into mechanical robots. In 1943 an article by Warren S. McCulloch and W. Pitts* appeared that suggested comparisons of computer elements with the neurological system of man.
The idea that machines could be given, in principle at least, the
capacity to imitate human behavior was appealing to such computer
people as A. M. Turing,† of Teddington, England. His machine was
conceived to handle general computational problems through use of
simple markings on a very long tape. When fed into the machine,
the tape moved along in steps, or blocks. Each block could be left
blank or it could have a check mark as one of a series of checks to
represent a letter or number. Thus a series of ten check marks in ten
blocks could represent the number ten. Another series of check
marks could carry instructions to the machine to change the markings
that were on the tape or to shift from one position of the tape to
another. The tape, which could carry all kinds of symbols and instructions that relate to real-life situations, could also carry instructions for changing the markings on the tape itself. The machine was
provided with erasers and markers with which to make changes on
the tape. What the machine did therefore depended in part on the
action that was called for by the portion of tape that was being
scanned at a particular time, and partly by what the machine had
been doing up to that time. There was a semblance of the machine
reacting to the environment (as recorded on the long tape being fed
to the machine) in a manner that was determined by the state of
the machine at that instant of time. By such reasoning and by assuming infinitely long tapes, it seemed possible, in principle at least,
to develop robots that could imitate some human activities. When
discussing genetic reproduction processes and the code characteristics
that are contained in long DNA and RNA molecules, one may recall the Turing machine and its long tape records.

McCulloch and Pitts examined the workings of neurons arranged
in simple circuitry and found some remarkable parallels with the
diode-operated circuitry of computer systems. It was very easy to
compare the input-output workings of neuronal circuits and to draw

* See References.
† See his article "Computing Machinery and Intelligence," in *Mind*, 59, 1950.
Also "On Computable Numbers, with an Application to the Entscheidungs-
problem," *Proceedings of the London Mathematical Society* (Sec. 2) 42, 1936.
Also "A Correction," ibid. 43, 1937.

circuits that were exact representations of simple on-off switch positions in combinations of switches. There were the receptor neurons and the effector neurons with the synapse between them. The receptor neurons could either be all of a kind in order to press their influence to fire the effector neurons, or some of the influence could be inhibitory and subtract from the total input. It was easy to duplicate with neurons the elements of computer circuitry that provide addition, subtraction, or multiplication functions. It was even plausible to add a new arrangement with feedback, illustrated in Fig. 20,

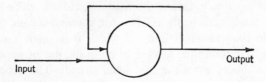

Fig. 20. Neuron with feedback.

whereby some semblance of positive feedback could make the neuronal circuit permanently alive. It did not seem farfetched to add more units and more complexities, until one might, in principle at least, visualize close parallels between the brain and mechanical-circuitry automatons. But as Singh points out, it is one thing to see parallels in the very simplest elements that make up neural versus mechanical systems and quite another to extend the parallels from microelements to the macrosystem. For it is even difficult to describe the nature of the phenomena with which the human nervous system is prepared to cope. Language is based on experience of *macroevents,* while the experiences themselves are the product of myriads of *microevents* that are much too small to be observed individually. An example is the ability of the brain to identify readily analogous geometrical patterns and the impossibility of giving unambiguous and complete verbal description of that simple visual faculty. It appears that future developments will derive principles of logic from neural examples rather than find neural explanations in the everyday logic that we build into machines.

While the pursuit of parallels between neural and mechanical circuitry reaches a point of diminishing returns rather quickly, one idea that was pointed out by Von Neumann brings important consequences. This has to do with the question of the dependability of neuronal function. As Von Neumann pointed out, we have to assume that neurons are not altogether dependable—that on occasion they may fail to initiate or to conduct a pulse. What are the consequences? If a neuronal circuit should have feedback characteristics of the type in Fig. 20, we can conceive of a situation developing in which failure can become extended to many neurons. A neuron that discharges without adequate cause can continue to misfire. Von Neumann addressed himself to this problem by assuming that every neuron might suffer the same degree of unreliability and that the failure would occur randomly among the neurons. How could a system of neurons be made sufficiently reliable for communication in a situation wherein the individual units of which it is made up all suffer unreliability? He found the answer to be in the use of multiple units or *bundles* of fibers instead of individual strands. The dependence is then on the behavior of the *majority* of fibers and not on the behavior of any one or a few. This represents another form of redundancy than that which we noted in connection with language use. It is a form that can be utilized to obtain any degree of reliability desired, despite unreliability of individual elements, providing the multiplexing of cables is carried far enough. But Von Neumann also included the warning quoted at the beginning of this chapter against depending too much on models such as these for explaining brain functions. In contrast with brain functions, the electronic computer operates by a series of steps, each taken sequentially. A mistake in any single step can change the end results very dramatically —in fact usually making the calculation useless.

Whether one regards the comparison of electromechanical machines and circuitry with neurological systems to have been successful or not, the effort to make comparisons was exceedingly useful for changing the attitudes of specialists in the one area toward specialists in the other area; that is, interest developed in exploring interrelationships that extend beyond one's own disciplinary specialty.* It was especially important that neurophysiologists sought a firmer base for their science in mathematical and electromechanical models.

---

* There were also current activities in Russia under A. N. Kolmogoroff, about which the American scientists were not well informed. There was, for example, Kolmogoroff's "Interpolation and Extrapolation von stationären Zufalligen Folgen," *Bull. Acad. Sci.,* USSR, *Ser. Math.* 5, 3–14 (1941).

CHAPTER 8

Perception and the Learning Process

> I think, therefore I am.
> René Descartes (1596–1650)

Because information and informational feedback have very great importance in the functioning of cybernetic systems, it will be helpful to pursue somewhat further the question of how sensory signals become meaningful information. Moreover, the concern in this chapter is not with how darkened circles cause relays to operate but with how man perceives changes in the world around him, changes to which he must respond properly or suffer consequences in one form or another.

The question of how man obtains knowledge about the world of which he is a part has engaged philosophers since time immemorial. As indicated in the quotation from Descartes, the very questioning of how we know what we know is inextricably interwoven with the why and wherefore of life itself. However, in this chapter we shall confine discussions to the more limited (if still unfathomed) subject of neurological processes related to epistemology.

Perception and its philosophical implications

In recent decades considerable information about perception has been obtained by the work of physiologists and from the newly developed disciplines of psychology and psychiatry. It would have been good to be able to say that we are now in possession of adequate information and satisfactory theories about the nature of perception, thinking, and mental processes generally, but such is not the case. For one thing, there has not been as much co-operative effort among the specialized disciplines as such studies require. Nor has it been easy to divest the studies of overdependence on the attitudes of the past.

Detailed studies of neurological processes of recent years have changed the picture only somewhat as to the physiological role of the sensory system. Anatomically it has been possible to identify the sensory receptors and to trace many of the neural interconnections leading to the central nervous system. It has been possible to analyze the physical form (that is, the electric pulses) of the "messages" that are sent by the sensory receptor organs to the central nervous system. By extensive testing of the effects of damage to the system and by subjecting the parts of the system to drugs, it has been possible to demonstrate a considerable degree of specialization of brain functions and regions. Nevertheless serious questions persist with respect to the fidelity of correspondence with which sensory organs respond to external stimuli, to add to the old questions of how far the senses can be trusted to reveal the exact nature of the world outside.

The difficulties increase as one proceeds from the intermediary sensory organs and functions to the perceptual processes whereby the central nervous system converts sensory messages into meanings and understanding. As Price philosophized several decades ago, perception that one personally experiences may develop as follows:

"When I see a tomato there is much that I can doubt. I can doubt whether it is a tomato that I am seeing and not a cleverly painted piece of wax. I can doubt whether there is any material there at all. Perhaps what I took for a tomato was really a reflection; perhaps I am even the victim of some hallucination. One thing, however, I cannot doubt: that there exists a red patch of round and somewhat bulgy shape, standing out from a background of other colour-patches, and having a certain visual depth, and that this whole field of colour is directly present to my consciousness. What the red patch is, whether a substance . . . or an event, whether it is physical or psychical or neither . . . we may doubt about. But that something is red and round then and there I cannot doubt."*

Of course Price is considering only that which comes from vision alone. In any real experience, more than one of the senses is likely

* Price, H. H., *Perception* (London: Methuen & Co. Ltd., 1932). Reprinted by permission of the publisher.

to come into play. The tomato becomes a tomato only as the senses of touch and taste join to declare that what we see is a tomato. Indeed the senses are not as often deceived as one might assume from such analyses. Nevertheless we recognize that the senses can lead one to error unless precautions are taken to bring in some tests. There can be what psychologists call *illusions*. When driving along an open road on a hot day, one frequently "sees" a lake of water ahead, which we call a mirage. The mirage is one of the serious problems of desert life. The cause of the mirage is the refraction of light rays coming from the sky. Refraction of light rays also accounts for the bent appearance of a straight stick that is partly immersed in water. In a sense, it is wrong to blame these inadequacies on the visual mechanism, for in each case the eye simply transmits a reasonably faithful image of the pattern of light rays that reach it; that is, the eye is not responsible for the refraction of light that takes place in the external world. In giving a deceptive message on the mirage or the bent stick, the eye is only serving as a faithful recorder of what itself receives.* On the other hand the illusory experience in the cinema, of seeing continuous motion whereas the projection of the film actually is made up of a rapidly moving series of still pictures, can be properly blamed as a limitation of the visual apparatus. The limitations also come in when one sees double as a result of excessive use of alcohol or drugs.

In the preceding quotation Price refers also to *hallucination* as a possible source of error, which represents an extreme state of illusion in that the object that is "seen" may not be there at all. (In veridical hallucination the experience is related to some real event, such as when one "sees" a person who has just died.) "Seeing" a snake or rats when drunk, "hearing" voices, being subject to apparitions when in a state of delirium or under the influence of drugs, or feeling pain in a leg that has been amputated may be in this class. There can be a variety of "misrepresentations" on the part of the eye that are more likely to be cases of error in the interpretive processes, such as when the actual size or nature of an object is misjudged because of the relationship to the background or the way it is located in relation to other objects. Philosophic minds sometimes assign the phrase *relativity of perception* to this form of illusion. An object may feel warm or cold depending on what the hand has

---

* This point seems to be disregarded by some psychologists.

touched just prior to that particular experience. The taste of a particular food varies considerably, depending on what has been tasted earlier.

The term *perception* originally had a rather broad meaning, implying any act or process of knowing objects, facts, or truths, whether by sense experience or by thought. It has been limited by psychologists to sensory processes involving objects external to the body, without, however, excluding the influence of judgment or experience. Said another way, perception is "sensation plus past experiences." Identical stimuli can yield quite different understanding, depending on the state of the body generally, the emotional and mental set, purposeful selection, experiences from the past, memory, attention, ego-defense functions, judgment, etc., that precede or accompany each stimulus. In other words perception has its component parts and perhaps sequential stages of development as well, while the "whole" perception also includes understanding of *causal relationship*.

Thus when one "perceives" an object that he says is a house or an animal, the implication is that there is actually a house or an animal in view. At this stage, all that the "perceiver" can really be sure of is that the eye receives a stimulus that is ordinarily associated with a house or an animal. Whether the house or animal is really there or not, the viewer experiences perceptual consciousness, admitting that the subject could be either real or an illusion or a hallucination. He knows (or is confident) that the stimulus arises from outside his body, emanating from the distant objects he thinks to be a house or an animal. There is, therefore, some process of profile matching or clue identification that participates in this recognition, arising from *within* the viewer and based on earlier experiences and on learning. This very rapid categorization, this intuitive "jumping to conclusions" may utilize a great many related aids derived both from the earlier experiences and background of the viewer and from the immediate background of the house or animal. There is, in other words, a "mental set," with which the viewer responds to the stimuli, that determines to some degree whether he "sees" a house or an animal or something else. This inner reaction of the viewer seems to be as necessary as is the external stimulus for the development even of the immediate reaction or the perceptual consciousness of what is going on; *that is, even the initial perceptual consciousness develops* only with a co-ordinated activity of the sensory receptors and the inner functions of the brain, utilizing earlier experiences and memory as a base.

Accepting this initial step as a combined, co-ordinated activity of the "sense data" and of contributions from the "inner" activities of the body, what completes the process of perception? It appears that there follows a more analytic process, in which judgment, comparison, selectivity of stimuli, modification of stimuli (say, by change of the viewer's position in relation to the object being viewed), and especially identification of a clearer *causal* relationship between object and stimulus all play a part.

The above discussion must not give the impression that the formation of perception follows a piecemeal assembly of parts or sequences. Indeed a whole movement, called *Gestalt psychology,** has taken shape within the past half century to emphasize the idea that perceptions are not built up out of discrete sensations or "particles of sensations." Instead we must recognize the existence of organizations and structures in experience that are integrated and difficult to split up into ultimate components. Perception and mental activities in general therefore derive significance from *the relationship to each other* of the parts that make up the total picture. (The phrase often used is "by differentiating from the continuum.") We shall go into this presently in more detail.

Mind and body: a modern view

Without including teleological implications, or implications of "purpose" in nature, the confusion and conflict of ideas about the nature of man and of knowledge seem to have given way to ideas that share certain features of the *oneness* proposed by the early Greek philosophers and especially by Aristotle twenty-three centuries ago. The revolutionary changes that came with the mechanical age and the age of reason seemed to upset these ideas and to suggest dramatically new categories for the animal-machine and even for the "man-machine." But the progress of psychology, psychiatry, and physiology have made it clear that we can no longer speak of the

---

* The word *Gestalt* is from the German meaning form, shape. Gestalt psychology was developed in Germany by the *Gestalt school* and by psychologists in Denmark and Austria.

mind as a mysterious entity that is simply lodged in a body/carrier. The mind and body cannot be separated, for the simple reason that they are not separate entities. Rather we seem to be forced to admit that

> ". . . the human organism is a conscious one and it is to this consciousness, the power of the organism with a sufficiently complex and developed brain to be aware of itself, its history and its environment, that we refer when we speak of 'mind.' Mind is not an entity or substance, but is a set of dispositions, faculties, activities, and tastes possessed by a human being."*

There are, of course, aspects of life such as locomotion and ingestion of food that on the surface appear to be altogether "physical," and aspects such as thinking that appear to be altogether "mental." As one pursues each, however, it becomes evident that the two categories are not separable. That is, the *mental functions* derive significance both from the structure and characteristics of the body and from memory of the experiences of the past to which the individual has been subjected. Also, every form of bodily activity seems to involve or have interrelation with some aspect of what is normally categorized as mental activity. On this premise the distinction and dualism that one seems to observe in mind/body relations represent only a superficial view of things, taking into account only the aspect that is the more obvious in any particular function or situation. Something of a distinction can be made in the phenomena associated with each type of experience and in what one may measure or fail to measure in each. There is the aspect of neuronal and of brain activity that one can probe by means of electrical instruments, such as when we measure the electric discharges that travel along a neuron. These may be thought of as being external, measurable, or at least detectable with physical instruments. In this way one could, for example, subject the ear to sound, and register on an oscilloscope the electric pulses that pass through the exposed nerves leading from the hearing organs to the central nervous system. There are, however, aspects of that hearing experience that are not measurable or registrable on an oscilloscope. These have to do with the association of that sound on the part of the hearer with other

---

* From Wyburn, Pickford, and Hirst, in References.

sounds, with other experiences of the past or present, which may produce an interpretation or an emotional experience that is totally unpredictable from anything one may have measured from the afferent neuron itself. Is the emotion that comes from sound a product, or direct effect, in the sense that the sound is the *cause* and the emotion the *effect?* Not directly, although there is usually some relationship. For example, suppose the ear is subjected to the sound of a gong every five minutes without there being any change in the sound intensity or quality. The neuronal discharges would probably be identical each time the sound is given to the ear, but the reaction of the hearer will vary enormously from the first gong to the one-hundredth. From a casual reaction to the first few soundings, there can develop indifference to further soundings; or there can develop strong emotions if the soundings are continued very long. In other words there is not a strictly cause-and-effect relationship between brain activity (or neural or sensory activity as one might measure these *externally*) and the conscious experiences, or emotions, or thought processes that are *internal* to the individual. The external and the internal phenomena seem to occur together as co-ordinated activities, each influencing the other. It is possible to direct the nature of that influence somewhat. For example, one can decide not to "hear" a particular sound and thereby greatly modify the nature of the awareness and effects of that sound as compared with the results if he were to concentrate on that sound.

Gestalt theory and the perception of form

At this point it will be useful to discuss some of the ideas that go under the name of *Gestalt theory*. For that we turn to philosopher-psychologist Max Wertheimer (1880–1943), who was born in Prague and spent his later years in the United States. Wertheimer was founder, with Wolfgang Köhler and Kurt Koffka, of the Gestalt school of psychology.* The general approach of the Gestalt theory may be stated in simplified form as follows: Most situations or experiences of which we become aware through the senses are made up of discrete parts, or elements. For example, any view to which the eyes may be exposed is likely to be made up of various objects and backgrounds. The over-all significance and impact of the whole situation or ex-

* See the book edited by Ellis, in References.

perience, however, is not determined by the simple summation of the individual intrinsic characteristics of the elements. The over-all situation or experience carries greater significance than can be accounted for by a mere summing up of the characteristics of each part. Each individual element acquires some of its significance from the part it plays in that particular, total situation.

Consider a room arrangement associated with a theatrical production and an identical arrangement located in a store window. The impressions that one associates with each piece of furniture differ very greatly in the two settings. For example, when in the store window, an empty chair remains only an empty chair, while that same chair may portray poignant human experiences in a play. Similar considerations apply to experiences that involve other senses. As Wertheimer states it, "There are wholes, the behavior of which is not determined by that of their individual elements, but where the part-processes are themselves determined by the intrinsic nature of the whole. It is the hope of Gestalt theory to determine the nature of such wholes." Gestalt theory is therefore concerned with the *approach* and *attitude* with which one comes to a situation.

The theory becomes useful for attacking certain problems of perception, one of which was posed by C. von Ehrenfels in connection with hearing and remembering a melody made up of six notes. The melody may be replayed in a different key, thus making the frequencies of the individual notes entirely different from the frequencies first heard. Yet the hearer will recognize the melody to be the same and he will assign an identical role to each note even though it may have a totally different frequency and quality from that first heard. There may be changes in the tempo or in the timing between notes, with the same results. To explain this, Ehrenfels proposed that each situation possesses, in addition to the elements that make up the situation, a *form-quality* (*Gestaltqualität,* he called it) that is present and is retained by the hearer despite transpositions of the situation. The same situation exists when we view photographs of an individual taken at different ages.

Gestalt theories include the viewer (the Ego) as a functional part of the "whole," or of "the total field." This requires that the environment and the organism be viewed as interacting with each other, so that the organism experiences continual change in its attitudes, striving, and feeling. The interactions are with other organisms as well, so that the members of a group work with a sense of awareness of the role of the group and of the whole.

With this approach the world is no longer like a "bundle of fragments" or the summation of a mass of discrete elements. Nor does it permit a dualism of body and mind. On meeting any situation, each individual brings to it a mental set, or *objective set,* which is determined by past experiences. One of the more interesting of the perceptive processes has to do with the recognition of *form.* How is it that the mind is able to recognize that certain forms the eye sees represent circles, whether they are large or small, near or far, in elliptic profile, alone or as part of an assembly? How is it that a face may be distorted, in profile or full face, formed out of dots or lines or in solid color, and yet be recognized as being a face? The geometric array, the colors, the relationships, and the intensity of stimulus that reaches the eye are rarely identical in any two observations, yet the perception is sure.

Psychologists have provided several guides for cataloguing tendencies in perception. Most situations or experiences involve a large number of stimuli or of possible sources of stimuli. The sensory system of the body is capable of giving attention to only a limited number of these at a time, however. This means that the mind can focus on only a limited number of stimuli or objects at a time, say up to a dozen or less. The mind will select a portion of the field of stimuli on which to focus, or pass successively from one portion to another. In each case the portion or part that is "in focus" stands out against a background that is diffuse and without clear definition. The stimuli then become organized in a figure/ground relationship, whether the stimuli are visual or arise from other senses.

There are a number of Gestalt principles or factors that are proposed to account for the forms that are perceived. Suppose that the eyes are exposed to a visual field containing a variety of dots, small crosses, and lines. By a process that is sometimes called *segregation and differentiation,* the eyes and mind quickly identify patterns and forms that are suggested by the various markings: (a) Dots that are close together spatially will be grouped together relationally. The effect is attributed to the factor of *proximity.* (b) In a mixture of markings, the ones that are alike will be seen as related. Here the effect is attributed to the factor of *similarity*. For example, in a field that includes crosses as well as other markings, the crosses may appear to stand out as a pattern either by this proximity to one another or by reason of similarity of form. This effect is often observed in a mixed group when the female dancers are seen separately in one pattern organization against a pattern of male dancers. (c) When similar markings lie equidistant along an imaginary line, the eyes will see a line and a direction. This is accounted for by assuming that there exists a *continuity factor,* or *direction.* (d) Markings will of course stand out differently when they *contrast* with each other. (e) When a field has a scattering of markings, the eyes will be drawn to portions that have a high concentration of markings. It is said that the eye is guided by the factor of *inclusiveness,* which draws attention to the highest concentration of stimuli. (f) In a field that includes many and diverse markings, a group that moves along without losing its pattern is distinguished from the rest by virtue of the factor of *common fate,* or *uniformity.* (g) If one has just been exposed to a particular pattern of stimuli, say one that resembles a dog or a star, he will be inclined to continue to see a dog or a star by means of the factor of *objective set.* (h) When a figure has most of the lines that outline a triangle or other pattern but lacks some portions, the eyes will "see" a full triangle or pattern by the factor of *closure.* (i) A pattern that has just appeared will take precedence over the rest by the factor of *recency.* (j) There are present other factors that are less clearly identifiable but that are present to influence the perception; these have been called factors of the *good Gestalt* or *good curve,* of *symmetry,* of *compactness,* and of *stability,* and are likely to be quite subjective.

Gestalt principles are not limited to vision. In fact the principles seem to apply to each one of the senses. Each note of music one hears is given a mental context or "background" in experiences, memory, and associations that goes well beyond the scope one might assign objectively to the note alone. Touch, movement, sight, sound join to give each perceptive experience a significance that goes beyond what one might obtain from only a simple adding up of the individual sensations, or "parts." Dance and music may combine to give a total sense of rhythm and composition and meaning that far surpasses the scope that might come by simply adding foot motion to notes of music. Conversely, within this Gestalt pattern of the total experience the individual movements of the foot and the individual notes of music have significances that greatly exceed what one might assign to each on a strictly objective basis.

"What the frog's eye tells the frog's brain"

Because of the emphasis that has been given to visual perception, it will be interesting to mention an article titled "What the Frog's Eye Tells the Frog's Brain."* The frog's eye has a uniform retina (without anything corresponding to the fovea of the human eye) with a connecting system of nerves going from the retina to the portion of the brain called the *colliculus* (and without further distribution in the brain as in the human system). Its eyes are stabilized in that they do not move to focus on a prey, but the frog will change its position as required to take in a new field of view. The frog seems to be responsive only to movement of food or prey, and it is assumed that it might starve to death even when surrounded by food, if there is no motion. The retina has about a million receptor rods and cones and about a half-million ganglion cells nearby in a single layer with about 2½ to 3½ million interconnecting neurons; that is, each rod or cone connects to many ganglion cells and each ganglion cell has connections with many thousands of receptors. These interconnections allow a great deal of overlap of adjacent ganglion cells. The connections of the ganglion cells to the brain are through a crossed optic nerve system (left eye to right side of brain, right eye to left side of brain).† The optic nerve contains about a half-million fibers, with roughly thirty times more unmyelinated than myelinated nerves densely packed and braided.

In the study referred to, it was decided to determine to what extent the frog eye is responsive to shapes, sizes, and movements, in addition to brightness of a spot. Probes were connected to various parts of the optic nerve or of the brain to record the

---

* By J. Y. Lettvin, H. R. Maturana, W. S. McCulloch, and W. H. Pitts, presented originally in *Proc. Inst. Radio Engr.*, 1959, *47*, pp. 1940–51. It is reproduced as Chapter 7 in the volume by Corning and Balaban, in References.
† This crossing is called the *optic chiasma*, from the Greek term for two lines placed crosswise.

reactions (by electrical amplification), and an aluminum hemisphere was mounted in front of the animal. Various objects could then be presented to the eye.

The study suggested that the eyes of the frog do some interpreting and organizing of the signals received at the retina, and that the message sent to the brain therefore incorporates a measure of perception of what has been "seen." What are the anatomical distinctions and functional characteristics that led them to this conclusion? There are four "sheets" in the brain, and groups of fibers of the optic nerves serve each sheet in such a way as to "map" the sheet in correspondence with a similar mapping of the retina.

It seems that "the output from the retina of the frog is a set of four distributed operations of the visual image." Each operation is entrusted to one of the sheets of the brain endings of the optic nerve. One set has to do with *detection of sharp edges and contrasts* against the background. Thus a nerve of this set does not discharge until the sharp edge of an object (which may be quite small and lighter or darker than the background) moves into the field and stops, at which time it discharges continuously regardless of the size of the object.

A second set has to do with detection of *net curvature* (convexity) of the object. Nerves in this category will not respond to the straight edge or flat face of a dark object. They do respond continuously to a convex object left in view or to the presence of an object that is darker than the background and moving on it. The third set, called *moving-edge detectors,* will respond only while the edge of an object (even a large object) is moving, the frequency of discharges increasing with the velocity with which the object moves. The fourth set, called *net dimming detectors,* is responsive to sudden reduction of illumination, producing discharges that are prolonged and regular with the dimming of light. The discharges increase as the illumination is reduced.

The functional features of the visual system of the frog seem to support the ideas offered by Gestalt psychology in the sense that such "perception" as evolves presumably is the product of the overlap of four sets of mappings on the "sheets" of neuronal endings in the brain. In the case of the human nervous system the anatomy is substantially different. Nevertheless the same techniques of amplifying and recording nerve discharge phenomena can shed considerable light on some of the neural processes related to learning and perception. We shall now jump from the frog to the human body in one large leap.

Electroencephalographic studies on humans

Electric-pulse discharges produced by stimuli in a neuron can be recorded by locating an electric probe on the nerve axon and amplifying and displaying the pulses by means of an oscilloscope. The neuron can then be given various forms of stimulation and the results analyzed with the oscilloscope. The pattern that shows on the oscilloscope can also be photographed. The research on the frog involved such studies, in which the probe could be located either on portions of the optic nerve or on parts of the brain exposed by opening the skull.

Although the results are usually better with an exposed brain, it is possible to record neural discharges without cutting into the scalp. If we place one electrode (which may be a metal plate) on the surface of the human scalp, and attach a second electrode to some other part of the head such as the ear lobe, a small voltage drop of the order of microvolts or a fraction of a microvolt can be detected between the two points of attachment. When this voltage is amplified about a million times and viewed on an oscilloscope, very interesting patterns are observed, which have the form of oscillations rather than individual pulses. The oscillations are roughly sinusoidal in form and have dominant or characteristic frequencies in the neighborhood of eight to thirteen cycles per second in the adult. Of course oscillations cannot represent pulses from individual neurons, since the electrode is located at a distance from all neurons. Rather, the oscillations represent an over-all statistical, integrated result of many neuronal discharges taking place between the two points where the electrodes are attached. Despite this diffused and uncertain feature, studies of this character have been very useful for revealing changes in brain function or at least changes in the oscillations that are recorded) as a function of body condition. The technique is called electroencephalography (or abbreviated as EEG). For example, by this method it is possible to expose the individual to various forms of experiences and stimuli and to observe the effects on the brain.

The frequencies of eight to thirteen cycles per second are usually called the *alpha* rhythm of brain waves for humans when they are awake but not engaged in visual activity. The frequencies may vary substantially among animals, although the general pattern may be about the same as in humans. Figure 21 illustrates the alpha-type oscillations in a human and the dramatic change that occurs when the eyes are opened. At first glance it will appear odd that greater neural activity (the eyes open and the mind working) should reduce the amplitude of the voltage so drastically. The explanation for this is that when the patient is quiet and not subject to any dominant neural activity, the neurons that do discharge tend to become synchronized and thereby to add up their voltages to produce a higher net voltage. When the eyes and brain are active, however, the greater neural activity also tends to throw the discharges more out of step with each other, causing many discharges to cancel out each other's influence at the location of the electrodes. This "blocking" of the alpha rhythm is for this reason sometimes referred to as desynchronization.* When the brain is exposed during surgery, it is possible to locate the electrodes directly in selected portions of the brain tissue, say the visual cortex, since the brain itself is not pain-sensitive. In one situation the patient was instructed to fixate on a small red dot in the center of a viewing screen, which caused immediate blocking (loss of alpha rhythm) lasting several seconds, as observed by five electrodes located in five different positions in the brain. Thereupon various sectors of the visual field were illuminated.

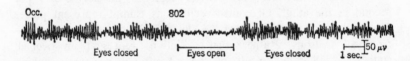

Fig. 21. Activation pattern. Blocking of the human alpha rhythm is produced by eye opening in a normal human subject. Derivation is from right occipital electrode referred to linked ears. (Courtesy of F. Morrell and The Rockefeller University Press)

* F. Morrell, among others reporting in the volume *The Neurosciences* (see References), gives some results of experiments addressed to such questions.

Illumination of the full screen caused alpha blocking at all electrodes, while with partial illumination only certain of the regions showed blocking. The interpretation is that blocking coincides with the beginning of brain activity involved in processing sensory signals. There is no evidence to suggest that the variations in the rhythm frequency are significant in any other way, such as serving as a code for the processing. The variations are simply a measure of the degree of synchronism or lack of synchronism in neuronal discharges.

Behavior of single cortical neurons

A neuron located in the brain has interconnections with many other neurons through synapses and through multiple branching, as we have seen. Keeping in mind the various cortical centers, one may ask to what extent a cell within the visual cortex is responsive also to other sensory stimuli, such as sound or touch. There is the question also of the nature of the neural pattern that develops from multiple stimuli, and whether it is possible to identify the nature of the stimulus from the pattern of the stimuli. For example, is there some kind of geometrical similarity between the object viewed and the neural pattern? Can the response pattern of neurons be changed so as to represent a "learning" process or "training" experience? The results of such tests suggest that a certain fraction of neurons of the visual cortex do indeed respond to other sensory stimuli and that while some neurons will not vary in their response to stimuli, others do vary as a result of what might be called conditioning experiences. That is, there appear to be in the cortex (a) some neurons that respond only to certain specific stimuli and maintain this form of sensitivity without essential change, (b) some neurons that are sensitive and responsive to sensory stimuli of more than one type, and (c) neurons that will vary their sensitivity and their response. Presumably the (b) variety help to integrate sensory information, while the (c) variety may be responsible for learning processes. (Of course the (b) and (c) types may be one and the same, for all we know.) At any rate, what we may regard as conditioning, or *learning,* on the part of a neuron is indicated by the ability of a neuron to *change its sensitivity or response* for extended periods of time when it is subjected to stimuli or treatment of any significant type.

With this in mind, note the results of some further experiments on changes in neuron sensitivity and response brought about by some form of conditioning. There are three patterns (or paradigms)

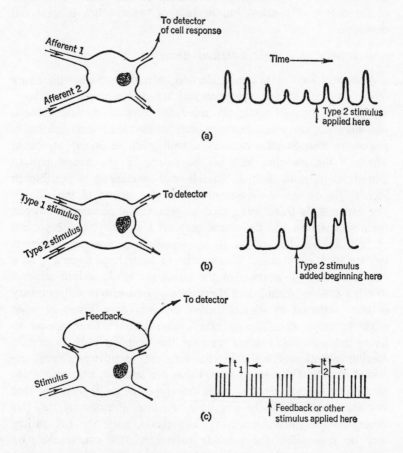

Fig. 22. Three methods for testing to determine if there are long-time effects (lasting days, weeks or years) on the sensitivity or response of neurons, which might be the equivalent of "learning." (From *Introduction to Natural Science.* Courtesy of Academic Press)

that the conditioning process and the sequential application of stimuli may take, as illustrated in Fig. 22.* The first is called habituation (Fig. 22 (a)), which simply involves repeating the application of a stimulus and observing changes in the response of the neuron. Usually the response decreases with monotonous repetition of stimulus, but can be restored by subjecting the neuron to another kind of stimulation or by giving it a rest period.

A second form of conditioning (Fig. 22 (b)) involves subjecting the neuron to *two stimuli*. Sometimes one form of stimulus has no effect in changing neuronal behavior, but the combination (or pairing) of that same stimulus with another form of stimulus produces quite different results. In this case it is customary to utilize two different afferent paths to the neuron for the two sources of stimuli. The first stimulus (the one that is normally ineffective in changing the response of the neuron) may be applied to one afferent path with an intensity that is enough to elicit a synaptic output pulse, while the second stimulus is imposed (as a train of pulses or in some other form) through the second afferent path. As illustrated in Fig. 22 (b) at times the effect of the original stimulus may be considerably modified for periods of days or longer.

A third type of conditioning or testing applies to cells that are themselves active in producing ongoing discharges but in which the nature of the discharges may be altered by *reinforcement*. As illustrated in Fig. 22 (c) a cell may on its own normally produce pulses with a rest period t_1. If an outside stimulus is applied during the rest period t_1, the activity could increase to produce pulses that occur at shorter time intervals t_2. The reinforcement or interference may take any of several forms, only two of which are illustrated in Fig. 22 (c). An outside stimulus can be applied through an afferent fiber. The magnitude of the stimulus and the phase relationship to the normal pulses of the cell can be varied. Or alternatively some of the normal output of the cell can be fed back to become an input stimulus. Depending on the phase relationship of the feedback pulse to the normal dis-

---

* The interested reader will find the chapter by Eric R. Kandel in *The Neurosciences* (see References) very useful for additional information on this exciting topic.

charges of the cell, the influence of the feedback can bring interference and reduction of output activity (negative feedback) or may enhance the activity (positive feedback). Since we know that the brain interconnections are enormously complex and permit reverberatory circuitry it is entirely feasible to include this form of reinforcement as a method by which neuronal cells may "learn" new behavior.

At this writing it is too early to say much about specific effects of conditioning on neuron performance characteristics. Suffice it to say that conditioning is possible, and the results observed do show some correlations with normal learning processes. It is not likely that individual neurons or small groups of cells can account for much of the processes we call perception, learning, emoting, or reasoning. Rather, accomplishment of these is dependent on the greater complexity and greater capabilities of whole masses of neurons and their interconnections.

What the brain does

The vast numbers of neurons that make up the cortical assembly, and their interconnections with the entire nervous system, afford capabilities that are new, subtle, and highly effective. The brain receives many kinds of signals from many kinds of stimuli, analyzes these signals with discrimination, takes action as required, and stores information for use in coping with future experiences. The brain is a very active part of the body, both as measured by its electrical activity and in terms of energy consumption. For while the brain constitutes only about 2% of body weight, it utilizes about 20% of the oxygen supplied to the body, even during its "inactive" periods. The muscles rise to this rate of oxygen consumption only during periods of intense activity, which we know cannot continue for too long. Perception of an event by the brain therefore results in *only a slight change* in a normally very active organ, and for a new event to be noticed at all it must produce an increase in visual or other signals of sufficient intensity to rise above the "noise" level of other activities.

We return to the question of how we perceive geometric form, spatial characteristics, and especially how we identify a square as a square and a face as a face regardless of size or color. The characteristics of the frog's eye offered some ideas but no specific guidance in this connection, while the studies on individual neurons offered much less information.

Electroencephalographic techniques have been very useful, however. In one series of tests* an electrode was located on the scalp of a man three centimeters above the inion (occipital protuberance of the skull), and the reference electrode was connected to his ear lobe. Once each second and for a total of from fifty to two hundred times for each test, a light was flashed to reveal to his view geometric patterns mounted on the wall. Meanwhile the voltages that were picked up by the electrodes were recorded on a continuing basis. These voltages represented not only the normal rhythmic potential wave forms but also the changes that occurred in the wave forms as a result of the visual experience. Figure 23 illustrates results that are highly significant. Here the subject

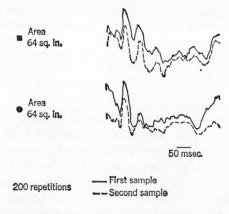

Area
64 sq. in.

Area
64 sq. in.

50 msec.

200 repetitions

——— First sample
— — Second sample

Fig. 23. Comparison of averaged response evoked by weak flash illuminating a white visual field containing either a black square or a circle, equated for area. Averages based on one hundred repetitions each. (From *The Neurosciences*. Courtesy of The Rockefeller University Press)

was exposed to a pattern of squares and a pattern of circles of equal area. The evoked potentials are clearly different for the

* See the chapter by E. R. John in *The Neurosciences* (in References).

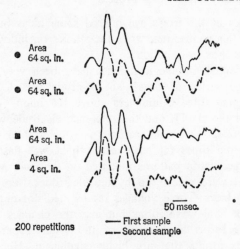

Area
64 sq. in.

Area
64 sq. in.

Area
64 sq. in.

Area
4 sq. in.

50 msec.

200 repetitions

—— First sample
－－ Second sample

Fig. 24. Comparison of averaged responses evoked by a weak flash illuminating a blank visual field containing either a square or a circle. Stimulus sequence was large circle, large square, large circle, small square. Note similarity of response to large and small squares. Each average based upon two hundred repetitions. (From *The Neurosciences.* Courtesy of The Rockefeller University Press)

two patterns, indicating that it is not size alone that makes the difference. The results shown in Fig. 24 are truly exciting, for while the potentials for the circles continue to differ from those evoked by the squares, there is a great similarity in the waves for the large and the very small squares; that is, recognition of the square patterns as being square clearly determines the shape of the potentials that are evoked by the perceptive process. A further test of evoked responses alternately utilized as a test pattern the words SQUARE and CIRCLE, which have the same number of letters and were given identical area of black portions of the words (Fig. 25). We note that the potentials evoked by the two words clearly differ.

It appears from these tests that the neural processes that accompany perception and recognition of a geometrical pattern are guided much more strongly by the *shape* of the pattern than they are by the size of the pattern. Much remains to be done to

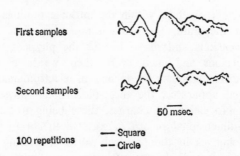

First samples

Second samples

50 msec.

100 repetitions   —— Square
                     —— Circle

Fig. 25. Comparison of averaged responses evoked by a weak flash illuminating the word SQUARE or CIRCLE printed in block letters. Total black area of both words was made equal. Note reproducibility of difference in responses between first samples (top) and second samples (bottom); each average based upon one hundred repetitions. (From *The Neurosciences.* Courtesy of The Rockefeller University Press)

reveal the neurological processes that come into play, but this close relationship of neural patterns to the shape of objects seems to support the principle of *isomorphism**** of Gestalt psychology.

Learning and memory

Thus far our concern has been largely with what is called *perception,* whereby neural discharges coming to the brain from peripheral sensory receptors convey some forms of information. The electroencephalographic records just described are related to processes that lead to perception. While whatever is perceived represents information during the instant of perception, to become useful knowledge the information must be retained and made useful *after* the perceived event has passed; that is, the dynamic electrical transformations that one observes on the oscilloscope, which are time-dependent and disappear very rapidly, must find a more permanent record such as is obtained by photographing the oscilloscope screen. *The time-variable image must be transformed into a spatially fixed photograph.*

How are fleeting perceptions made more durable? Obviously they

* The Greek *iso* means *equal, alike, the same; morphe,* also Greek, means *form.*

must be retained somehow within the intricate foldings and neurons that make up the brain. The brain is an organ composed of tissue that has dimensions and mass, just as the physical world outside us has dimensions and mass. Here, then, we have a remarkable series of transformations: By means of electromagnetic radiation and the visual apparatus, the three-dimensional physical world is transformed into electric discharges, these being transformed again into a three-dimensional record of sorts in the brain tissue. Moreover, rapid changes in the physical world or fleeting glances that give time-dependent discharges are transformed into relatively permanent three-dimensional patterns. Therefore knowledge and memory represent conversion of information that has both spatial characteristics and time-dependent characteristics into a spatial record in the brain. One might compare the transformations with those that take place in television, wherein a view of physical objects is transformed by electromagnetic waves into the movements of an electron beam that records on a physical screen. There is a very major difference in favor of the brain, however. For while the television screen records, and loses each scene one after another, the brain has the capability to record each scene, one after another, and to retain awareness of the time-dependent characteristics of each scene as well as the time sequence of the received information; that is, the mind includes also capabilities like those of a magnetic tape, which is capable of holding the record intact and available for recall as needed. In the same way, the mind is prepared to recall the stored information on demand even after long periods of dormancy and even if on occasion the individual becomes subject to shock, anesthesia, or new experiences, or suffers the ravages of time. The code by which sensory messages are transformed to become perception or knowledge is not known to us. Nor are we any better off with respect to the code by which perceptions are transformed to become memory. The memory trace is called the *engram.** The search for the code and characteristics of the engram has been fruitless thus far. Just as the associated electric activity and mental images of a house or automobile are completely different from the house or automobile, so there may

---

* The term *engram* was proposed in 1904 by Richard Semon, who believed that experiences do leave a discrete memory trace within the nervous system and that this trace might have a chemical nature.

be present entirely new phenomena that produce an engram from perception.

We do know that certain portions of the brain seem to house engrams related to specific learning tasks. For example, lesions in the visual cortex of rats will affect their visual-discrimination learning only. On the other hand, destruction of any part of the rat's brain will damage trial-and-error alley-maze learning. While complete destruction of the visual cortex makes a rat incapable of learning a task involving form discrimination, if even as little as one sixtieth of that cortex is left intact the rat is capable of learning in a normal fashion.

Experiments involving brain lesions have given considerable information on the relationship of learning ability and memory to the various portions of the brain. Again using ability for visual discrimination as a criterion, tests on monkeys showed that the *degree* of training has an influence on the amount of brain tissue that becomes involved in learning.* A monkey was trained to perform to a criterion of 90% correct responses in thirty trials on one visual-discrimination task. The same monkey was trained also for a second visual-discrimination task, but in this case it was given several hundred trials in *addition* to the training required to achieve the criterion of 90% correct. When some of the brain was thereafter removed, it was found that only the memory for the task that had had extra training was still retained by the animal. It is possible that additional learning tends to involve a larger area of the brain; that is, the substrate of the brain involved in discrimination learning tends to spread out to engage larger areas of the brain. A mechanism of this type (involving extension of substrate) could possibly also account for the ability of people to remember events of the distant past while quickly forgetting the immediate past.

An aspect of brain function that has been observed in many clinical cases has to do with the ability of the damaged brain to relearn functions and for other portions of the brain to take over functions that were lost through a lesion. These and other experiences support the idea that activities that establish the engram

---

* See the chapter by K. L. Chow in *The Neurosciences* (in References) for a review of the effects of ablation.

are dynamic in nature and that brain function cannot be represented by a rigid model of neuronal interconnections and static memory sites.

We recall that the brain has both left and right halves, and that there is a crossing of nerve trunks so that the right half of the brain is usually involved with the functions of the left side of the body and the left half of the brain with the right side of the body. How are these involved in the learning and memory processes? The two hemispheres of the vertebrate brain are actually separated anatomically except for some connecting fibers. In the case of monkeys, complete separation of the hemispheres down through the midbrain seems to introduce few difficulties.* Extending the division into the tegmentum, pons, and cerebellum has more effect on the monkey's stability and attitude. The experiments show that, when thus separated, the two halves of the body and brain are independent of each other and act as almost separate domains with respect to sensing, perceiving, thinking, and remembering.* Under these conditions the brain loses the ability to integrate the activities of one side with those of the other. For example, when a normal subject sees an object on the left side of his nose with the left eye and then the object is transferred to the right side, he has no difficulty in recognizing that this is the same object. With the split-brain syndrome, however, the two become totally unrelated; he would not recognize the object as being the same one that he saw with his other side. Memory that develops on one side remains on that side of the bisected brain.

The search for the engram

What is the nature of the *engram?* Or perhaps we should ask, what are the characteristics that engrams may have? The search for the engram has involved experiments on many insects, animals, and human subjects. Its presence is sensed in the simplest act of almost the simplest forms of living organisms. Its influence is present with our every movement of hand and foot, in that the movements involve controls that utilize experience and memory. Even-more-complex interrelationships, whose significances vary with every new situation, appear in the use of symbols, abstract thought,

* See the chapter by R. W. Sperry in *The Neurosciences* (see References).

and language. These demand general involvement of the brain, and of reasoning and perceptual capabilities, and contradict the idea that a specific point of the brain is entrusted with a specific memory function.

The study of how external conditions and experiences influence memory began with the German Hermann Ebbinghaus, in the middle of the nineteenth century. A number of Americans sought unsuccessfully for behavioristic explanations of learning and memory by looking for a relationship between stimulus response and the past behavior of an animal or human being. The Russian physiologst Ivan Pavlov was the first to stress the importance of the neural phenomena in the brain as responsible for learning and memory. The work he initiated is being continued in many parts of the world. The American psychologist K. S. Lashley searched many years for the engram, in this case including extensive training of animals and dissecting of brains to correlate learning with specific brain tissue. His search, which sought answers in neurophysiological processes, was not successful in its main objective. More recently the search has shifted toward biochemical processes as providing the answer, with the thought that perhaps the learning process produces a chemical change in one or more nerve cells in the brain. In 1950 the American psychologists J. J. Katz and W. C. Halstead* theorized that the engram might be related to changes in the nucleic acids of a single cell. During 1962 and 1963, the Swedish biologist Holger Hydén found ribonucleic acid (RNA) constituents that seemed to act as a "memory molecule." Was it a case of the RNA molecules "remembering" the organism's own life experiences while the DNA code represented the "memory" of the organism's progenitors? Was this therefore a process by which both the code obtained from DNA molecules and the current experiences of the organism became implanted in the RNA molecules? The implications are tremendous.

Hydén developed very delicate techniques for removing protoplasm from individual cells of the nervous system and analyzing it by microanalytic techniques for possible changes in the RNA mole-

---

* "Protein organization and mental functions," *Comp. Psychol. Monographs,* 20, pp. 1–38, 1950.

cules.* Working with two groups of rats, he trained one group to balance on a taut wire in order to reach food. The second group was given passive exercise that did not include balancing on the wire. On examining for the RNA concentration in cells taken from animals of each group, Hydén observed qualitative differences in the nuclear RNA taken from the animals trained to balance on the taut wire. His next findings, now on humans, revealed that the gross RNA concentration increases from birth until age forty, after which it remains constant until it decreases rapidly after age sixty.

We see, therefore, that the research of the past several decades on the brain and on mental processes has followed two directions, the one attempting to study behavior without too much attention to the behaving organism itself, the second attempting to correlate behavioral or psychological characteristics of animals and humans with tissue of the central nervous system. It is the latter approach that is receiving the greatest amount of attention at this writing.

To continue exploring the role of RNA let us suppose that some of the newly produced RNA molecules are transferred as an extract from the cells of a highly trained animal to a less-trained animal. Would the second, recipient animal thereby acquire some of the benefits of the training given to the donor animal? The experiments that are in progress seem to suggest that there are some transferred benefits, but there are not yet sufficient data to prove or disprove the idea. Experiments are underway on both invertebrates and vertebrates. Among the most interesting of the first category have been studies on the planarian, which is a fragile, common fresh-water flatworm of about one inch in length.† Although this creature has a very rudimentary brain, it is capable of fairly complicated behavior, and since 1920 has been shown to be capable of being trained to do such things as crawling along

---

* Refer to the chapter on "The Modern Search for the Engram," by James V. McConnell in the volume by Corning and Balaban and to the chapter on "The Enhancement of Learning by Drugs and the Transfer of Learning by Macromolecules," by G. C. Quarton in *The Neurosciences* (both in References) for more details. See also two chapters by Hydén in *The Neurosciences*.

† See the chapters by E. M. Eisenstein in *The Neurosciences* (in References) for details. Also, *Scientific American* frequently has articles on the nervous system.

a wire to reach food. The Canadian psychologist D. O. Hebb and the Australian John Eccles had postulated that the process of learning possibly changed conditions at the synapse. The planarian does have the simplest form of synapse, of a type that had been postulated and therefore is very suitable for use in these tests. There is the additional factor that when a planarian is cut in half transversely, the head portion grows a new tail and the tail portion a new head to return both pairs to the original size. McConnell and an associate, Robert Thompson, trained the worm to contract vigorously when subjected to certain light and electric-shock conditions. On cutting the worm in half, to their surprise both the generated halves—the tail portion with its new head and the old head portion with its new tail—showed almost perfect retention of the learning. The retention was there even when the worm was cut up into thirds and fourths. It seemed, therefore, that whatever corresponded to the engram was spread throughout the whole body of the worm.

After Hydén introduced the idea of RNA relationship to learning, tests with the planarian were continued by E. Roy John and William Corning. The worms were trained and cut as before. This time, however, some of the halves were allowed to regenerate in ordinary water while others were placed in water that contained a weak solution of ribonuclease (which is an enzyme that breaks up RNA by hydrolysis). On testing, while the head portions and tail portions that had regenerated in pond water and the head portions that had regenerated in the ribonuclease solution all retained the training, the tail portions that had regenerated in ribonuclease showed almost complete loss of learning, as though the memory had been erased by the hydrolysis of RNA.

Next McConnell succeeded in getting untrained planarians to cannibalize trained planarians, thus "injecting" some of the RNA from trained animals into the untrained (as well as some RNA from untrained into trained animals as controls). When the "cannibals" were then subjected to the same form of training, those that had consumed the trained planarians showed very much faster response to training than did the others.

There continue to be experiments also on rats. The evidence remains inconclusive at this time as to the basic mechanisms of the phenomena that have been observed. There has been enough revealed, however, to encourage some non-scientists and non-scientific literature to postulate that before long it will be possible to develop supermen by ingesting extracts and pills rather than depending altogether on schooling or genetic factors!

By way of summary and conjecture

Our current ideas on perception and on mind and matter have taken over twenty-four centuries to reach the present stage. There have been a number of transitions from one historical period to another that deserve more attention than we have given them. In perspective it is possible to identify a fairly normal, if slow, development of the successive phases. Each new phase has tended to emphasize an aspect that had been neglected up to its own time, and in turn each has overemphasized its own contribution to the extent of prejudicing progress in other directions.

The Greek period offered remarkable sensitivity to, and appreciation of, a wide variety of abstract concepts. Some of them saw many opposites in life—the "good" and the "evil," the one against the many, the harmonious against the lack of harmony, love against strife. Others emphasized that there was never love alone or strife alone; or black alone without the presence of some white, and the converse. A few had awareness of a basic unity in nature that reached deeper than the superficial contrasts, an underlying unity that might apply both to mind and to matter as well. To the atomists things were matter, and matter was alive. To others the spirit and the mind, along with the perfection of the sphere and the circle, went beyond matter. Not until after the Renaissance, with the coming of the machine age, was it possible to break away from the overpowering influence of these abstract concepts and to entertain new thinking.

There came next the "new thinking" of the machine age. In the spirit of the determinism that characterized that age, it seemed possible to find "machine" answers to body functions. Certainly muscle and body movement had great similarity to the parameters that were taken into account in the design of a machine—forces, inertia, leverage, speed of movement, energy required, etc. The machines of Descartes's day had to have external controls and energy input, and so it was not difficult for him to conceive of the body as a passive muscular machine that also required a separate and distinct

"motive faculty," called the "soul." Since the "motive faculty" had
no corresponding element in the machine, a duality of mind and body
seemed both unavoidable and acceptable. With all his willingness to
break from tradition, Descartes could not envision a mechanistic
view of consciousness nor deny the existence of consciousness as a
major aspect of his own human experience. The French physician-
botanist-philosopher Julien de La Mettrie (1709–51) found less
difficulty in envisioning that a machine-animal or machine-body
could also be capable of thinking. He elevated matter from being
thought of as base, inanimate material, by observing that inanimate
matter could, when properly organized, produce unseen electric currents and electromagnetic fields. The discovery by the Swiss physi-
cian-physiologist-anatomist Albrecht von Haller (1708–77) that the
heart muscle possessed some "inherent and intrinsic force" that
enabled the heart to function without dependence on the brain,
seemed to support de La Mettrie.

From our own observations we are driven to acceptance of the
idea that perception and knowledge involve a series of co-operative,
participating, co-ordinated features and activities. For receiving information from the world outside, the body is equipped with a sensory
system that is sensitive to certain changes and conditions in that
outside world. Of course there are far more phenomena involving
light and sound frequencies, temperatures, electromagnetic fields,
etc., to which we are not sensitive or responsive. The particular sen-
sitivities that we do enjoy have evolved over time and continue to
be maintained and modified through genetic mediation. But sensory
messages that go beyond those that produce reflex response achieve
significance only as the inner workings of the brain and "mind"
give them meaning by discriminating them one from another, and
relating them to each other and to earlier messages. This latter function, in turn, is determined by a host of earlier experiences that
accumulate from the genetic past and from the beginning of infancy.
Not the least of the contributing factors to this capability derives
from the cultural and language environment of the individual who
must do the perceiving.

The encephalographic studies of brain waves and neural responses
evoked by visual forms, as well as the research results that associate
learning with RNA molecules, are of very great interest. But prom-
ising as they are of new ideas on the basis of learning and of

memory, we are forced to recall the warning to the effect that our observations of neural phenomena continue to be limited to gross, integrated effects. Norbert Wiener was among those who considered the possibility that the alpha rhythm represents the synchronized summation of short-range microradiation of individual neurons. Under suitable conditions it is possible even for such short-range radiation to synchronize and to produce gross measurable effects such as the alpha rhythm.

Wiener also dared to suggest the nucleic acid molecules (of which DNA and RNA or their complexes are of principal interest) as sources of the microradiation. Within the semicrystalline fluids of the cell interior, it is conjectured, these molecules could have highly specific distributions of frequencies. Presumably the learning process may alter the spectral distributions of frequencies, thus making the nucleic acid the memory unit, as suggested by some of the experiments just described. Conjecture though this is, the idea that some day nucleic acids may serve as memory units for computers did not seem altogether out of reason.*

And so with an all-too-brief historical review and some reporting on the behavior of neurons and of the brain in "learning" operations, we have arrived at questions and research activities that are currently among the most exciting in history. It is hoped that the reader will have achieved enough interest, familiarity, and excitement to pursue current experiments that are attempting to identify the "engram" with biochemical transformations involving RNA molecules. For indeed any device that stores memory and returns it again in due time to modify succeeding experiences constitutes feedback of the most important kind in cybernetic systems.

* See "A Tribute to Norbert Wiener," by Gordon E. Olson and J. P. Schadé, in *Cybernetics of the Nervous System,* edited by the late Norbert Wiener and J. P. Schadé (Amsterdam: Elsevier Publishing Co., 1965).

CHAPTER 9

Cybernetics in Human and Ecological Situations

"Here I need only mention the fact that cybernetics is likely to reveal a great number of interesting and suggestive parallelisms between machine and brain and society. And it can provide the common language by which discoveries in one branch can readily be made use of in the others."*

W. Ross Ashby

We turn now to examine a variety of situations that lend themselves to analysis through the systems, cybernetic, approach. As has been noted earlier, while only rarely does this approach provide complete answers, the reader will recognize that in the examples, complete answers have not been available by any other means either. Moreover, the *attitude* and the emphasis on *feedback interrelationships* that the concepts of cybernetics demand of the investigator can spell the difference between superficial and probing investigation of a situation. We noted also that in most situations (other than simple electromechanical systems) it is very difficult to identify all the interrelationships that exist among the elements and subsystems, and even more difficult to make quantitative analyses. Nevertheless it is often possible to learn whether the *net result* of feedback influences is negative or positive. If, because of "damping" effects and feedback, the net influence is negative feedback by even a minute amount, the system is likely to remain stable. But if the net influence of feedback is positive and continues positive by even a very small amount, the excursions and instabilities will increase until the system itself is finally changed or destroyed.

* From *An Introduction to Cybernetics* (London: Chapman and Hall, 1961).

Example of a communications system

With only minor modifications, the diagram of Fig. 9 can represent a system for communication of information. Figure 26 illustrates

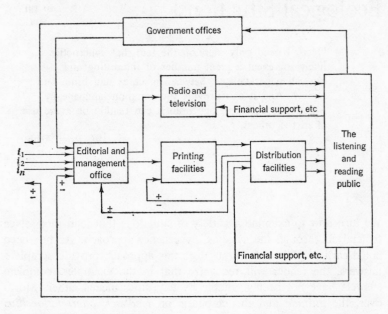

Fig. 26. Schematic representation of a system for communicating news to the public. (From *Introduction to Natural Science*. Courtesy of Academic Press)

some of the elements that enter into a system for communicating news to the general public. News may be collected from many areas and reported as input (i_1, i_2, ... i_n) to the editorial offices of a news agency. There will be both public and government influences, and sources of information bearing on the editorial and management offices, much of it in the form of feedback reaction to the news reports. The listening and reading public applies "feedback" influence through financial support (or lack of support) of the broadcast and publishing services, and there could be circuitous pressures brought to bear on the government and on other institutions as well. The constraints in such a system are many. They arise from national and local government policies; from electrical, chemical, and mechanical limitations; from the cultural habits and educational levels of communities; and from economic considerations. As a total result, such a communications system becomes not a simple amplifier and distributor of news information, but a combination system for receiving, interpreting, modifying, distorting, and even falsifying, the news, with built-in restraints and objectives and occasional arguments in courts of law.

Any one of the multiple input signals may suddenly overshadow all other input signals and bring about a violent response in either the forward channels or the feedback channels. Such a disturbance might be an act of war, a strike, a catastrophe, or an event that is especially exciting, such as one of the early trips to the moon. However, under normal circumstances there is a *statistical character* to the sum total of the inputs which is not overly influenced by any one item.

The genetic code and the production of proteins

Undoubtedly the most remarkable examples of uniqueness, complexity, and effectiveness in the informational and control elements of cybernetic systems are found in the genetic code of living cells. How the genetic code became established and grew in complexity we cannot guess. Suffice it to say that the code prescribes the directions for protoplasmic development in such a way as to differentiate each of the three million species of living organisms one from another. Moreover, the differentiation of one species from another is made possible by producing thousands of different kinds of proteins, enzymes, and molecular forms within each animal body—each kind of protein or cell or tissue having the correct structural and numerical ratio to the others. We marvel that the coding mechanism permits such great variety, and that it is so effective as to assure that each cell divides and multiplies in the image of the original cell.

For example, in 1912 at the Rockefeller Institute (now Rockefeller University) a research team guided by Alexis Carrel removed cells from the heart of a living chick embryo and placed them in a nutrient solution. The cells lived and multiplied many times as new food was made available from time to time. The excess of cells was removed and discarded periodically. When the experiment was terminated in 1939 the cells were still alive and flourishing. The single cell that was transplanted in 1912 divided once every two days. Therefore during the experimental period of twenty-seven years, 10^{1500} new cells could have been produced. Considering that the number of electrons in the entire universe is postulated to be not greater than 10^{90}, it is seen that the number of cell divisions that can occur in a lifetime is beyond comprehension.

The most remarkable aspect of all this has to do with the similarity of the cells that were produced in the twenty-seventh year to the first cell. Surely this depended on very precise information being available to the process, and on effective controls for use of the information.

We have learned since then that deoxyribonucleic acid (or DNA) molecules, which are associated with genic material and found in great numbers in the nucleus of the living cell, do indeed contain coded information that prescribes the process of growth. The process is designed, among other functions, to select the correct amino acids from among the twenty that make up protoplasm. In the DNA molecule, the code utilizes four different molecules (bases) as the elements, and the *order* in which any three of the four appear in relation to each other determines a *code bit* representing a particular amino acid.* That is, the *sequence* of the nitrogenous bases that make up the long DNA molecule is the main device that prescribes the nature of the protein molecules that are synthesized. Since there are many thousands of *kinds* of protein molecules, there must be correspondingly many kinds of codes.

The process as envisioned at the present time is that the DNA molecules first transfer the code to a variety of messenger-RNA and transfer-RNA molecules (ribonucleic acids) in the form of complementary codes that have sequences of four bases also. The messenger-RNA molecules travel to the sites of ribosomes of the cell, where protein synthesis takes place, while the transfer-RNA molecules go to the pool of amino acids to select the correct amino acid to bring to the ribosomes for synthesis to produce protein molecules.

The details of the process for the production of proteins have not yet been revealed. Nevertheless it is useful to postulate what might be the process in the context of our present interest. One highly conjectural scheme is presented in Fig. 27. The figure follows some-

---

* The interested reader can obtain details from *Introduction to Natural Science*, Part II, by Parsegian et al.

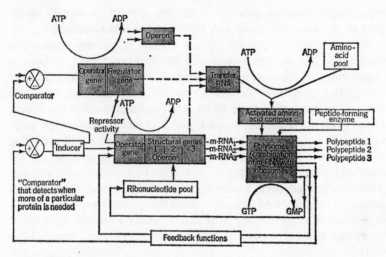

Fig. 27. Postulated control system for synthesis of proteins, utilizing some concepts of the Jacob-Monod scheme. The shaded blocks represent aspects that include hereditary characteristics of the genes. The comparator at upper left may detect a need to inhibit production of a particular type of protein and initiates repressor activity through the center "operon circuit." The lower left comparator, in contrast, detects a need to induce production of more of another protein. (From *Introduction to Natural Science.* Courtesy of Academic Press)

what the approach first proposed by Jacob and Monod.* In this scheme the DNA is called the *structural gene* containing the full code for each protein. Since most of the DNA is located within the nucleus of a cell, and protein synthesis takes place in the cytoplasm, we must call for the messenger RNA (or m-RNA) to convey the code and to help the synthesis. The messenger-RNA is itself produced at the site of the DNA molecule, and so there is involved here what Jacob and Monod have called an *operator* function, initiated at specific points on the DNA strand. The genes whose activity is co-ordinated in messenger-RNA synthesis form an *operon;* that is, the operon is made up of an operator gene that functions with one or more structural genes. There is also a regulatory function ex-

---

* François Jacob and Jacques Monod, "Genetic Regulatory Mechanisms in the Synthesis of Proteins," *J. Mol. Biology* 3, 318–56 (1961). A review article.

ercised by a *regulator gene* that promotes or restrains activity on the part of the operator genes and hence of the whole operon.

According to Fig. 27, the normal control of protein synthesis is directed by the operon box at the center of the figure, which is responsible for producing messenger RNA and possibly transfer RNA. The m-RNA molecules go to the ribosome sites and may form polysomes, while the transfer-RNA molecules select the proper amino acids from the amino-acid pool and carry them to the polysomes. The polypeptides (proteins) are thereby synthesized according to the genetic information contained in the genic material of the structural genes of the operon. We note that nucleotides are also produced that go back to the operon site from which more RNA molecules are produced to replace those that leave the site as m-RNA or t-RNA. Energy for the synthesis is made available by various phosphate-exchange reactions indicated as ATP→ADP and GTP→ GMP.*

We have assumed that the production of each type of protein requires the presence of a specific m-RNA molecule. (It may also be that one m-RNA is required for the synthesis of each individual protein.) It is understandable, therefore, that the correct proportion of types of proteins will be synthesized only if the correct proportion of m-RNA molecules is made available. It is this latter function, which is difficult to understand and to explain, to which the remainder of Fig. 27 is addressed.

The process postulated by Fig. 27 for this control of m-RNA synthesis is shown to require the services of the structural genes and the operator genes. These, however, require additional regulation and control of either of two kinds: As a result of "feedback" information or from other causes, a "comparator" (lower one of the two at the left of Fig. 27) may detect the need for synthesis of a particular type of protein. It can "induce" the operator and structural genes of the central operon group to proceed with synthesis of that RNA molecule. Alternatively, there may be need to restrain that synthesis through the "comparator" at the upper left. That comparator, through its operator and regulator genes, initiates repressor activity to restrain or guide the synthesis of specific RNA molecules. The control of the relative numbers of RNA molecules thereby controls the ratio of protein types that are synthesized.

* See Parsegion et al., Part II, for the reactions.

The figure also shows dotted lines between the regulator genes, the transfer-RNA box, and the operon box. The feedback loops also are included. These, as well as the entire Fig. 27 represent mainly a gesture of recognition that there are a great many very close interrelationships among the functions, rather than suggesting that we have specific knowledge that the interrelationships must take these forms.

Processes for genetic change

The main purpose of the processes just described for the synthesis of proteins is maintenance of the pattern of the cell without change. This requires rather strong feedback, and apparently this is provided by the code contained in DNA and by the process just discussed. In the case of the organism as a whole, the situation is not quite the same. Each member of a human species differs significantly from every other member of the species. Each member is subject to environmental influences that affect his body in one way or another, in some cases the effect being on the hereditary genes (as due to chemical or radiation effects). Each member is a product of the sexual union of two different individuals. Each in turn will join in sexual union with another member (who is distinctly different) to produce progeny. Here is a situation that permits the control mechanisms to retain the principal characteristics of the species, yet assures that there will be some changes in those characteristics as well.

Figure 28 offers what might be a systems diagram to represent this situation. The center boxes represent the sum total of people, characteristics, and environmental relationships that exist. The input to these is from the left, from earlier generations. As noted at the top, there are some positive-feedback influences, but the dominant influence is of negative variety, which maintains the existing patterns. At the lower left, however, we have suggested the introduction of one new genetic feature which is "favored" and enhanced by means of positive feedback. If the positive feedback continues, there is a possibility that this new feature will produce a new organism, new either in some structural or some functional characteristics.

On ecological applications

We ordinarily think of living organisms as being products of the earth environment, and Chapter 10 will emphasize that aspect. Since

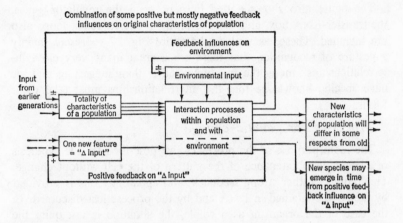

Fig. 28. A "systems feedback" representation of evolutionary changes. A new feature, called "Δ input," introduced in one generation, can, if there are positive-feedback influences, ultimately build up to give rise to a new species. (From *Introduction to Natural Science*. Courtesy of Academic Press)

man learned to make jinns of the materials and energy resources of the earth to serve his commerce and his whims, however, the influence is no longer unidirectional.

Within the past decade the world has awakened to the realization that the capability and quality of our earth system are being seriously prejudiced at a time when the population load on the earth's resources is increasing very rapidly. The reasons are that the materials and energy resources of the earth that make possible modern civilization are being converted into waste and pollution, some of it exceedingly toxic to man himself. There is required a major turnabout in social attitudes and more-conservative use of the resources, if the many generations yet to come are to have available to them materials with which to maintain viable societies. The approach of cybernetics is well suited to this analysis, and the remainder of this chapter will deal with that subject.

Ecological damage takes many forms. Every boiler or engine producing useful mechanical or electric energy through combustion of coal, oil, or natural gas is likely to spew carbon monoxide, sulfur compounds, nitrogen compounds, hydrocarbons, and particulates into the atmosphere unless these contaminants are purposely removed before exhausting the waste gases. The burning of gasoline may add lead and other hydrocarbons. The pollutants have made the atmosphere above large urban centers a serious health hazard to the people, and caused billions of dollars of loss to the nation through their corrosive action on buildings and on equipment.

Liquid wastes from industrial and commercial operations and from communities have rendered the rivers and lakes of most nations unfit for human use and no longer suitable for fish of desirable types. The pouring of toxic materials such as mercury into the waters has made fish such as salmon much less safe for use as food for humans, because they accumulate the mercury. Indiscriminate use of organochloride pesticides such as DDT has destroyed what may be called the "ecological balance" of many lands and waterways and has made some species of bird life almost extinct. The oceans are said to be rapidly turning into cesspools both as a result of the wastes pouring into them from land areas and as a result of spillage of oil and dumping of solid wastes into the seas.

Pollution and pollutants obviously represent good earth materials that because of mismanagement end up in the wrong places. The mines from which metal ores, coal, and other minerals are obtained, are being worked to depletion, and the land itself made desolate and unproductive in the process. The processed materials find their way into machines, automobiles, pots and pans, and all the other products that nations consume. Too often the chemicals used for their production become waste effluents into waterways, while the manufactured products ultimately find their way into dumps or into incinerators, from which they can no longer be recovered or reused.

It is imperative, if long-range viability for human society is to be assured, that there be curbs on the prodigality of "advanced" nations especially. For example, the population of the United States, constituting only 6% of the world's population, consumes 40% of the world's productivity and 35% of the world's material resources. The solution lies in conservation through recovery and recycling of minerals and organic materials, both to avoid early depletion of scarce materials and to avoid making toxic contaminants and waste out of good, useful materials.

What about the energy that must be used for recovery and recycling? The fact is that there is inadequate energy even now for the needs of populations. The principal sources of energy are fossil fuels—coal, oil, and natural gas—which are in short supply and also the major causes of pollution. The pollution they produce can be reduced, but only at the cost of burning still-more fuel through which to obtain energy for removing the pollutants before exhausting into the atmosphere. The process, then, has the elements of positive feedback, which causes depletion of the fossil-fuel reserves that much more quickly.

The more unfortunate aspect of this rapid depletion will be felt by the generations to come, who will have every reason to curse our prodigality. The reason is that the coal and oil could have had greater value as raw materials for chemical products than they have as inefficient sources of energy. However, until nuclear-energy plants are made suitable for incorporation within urban and industrial complexes, there is not likely to be much change in the situation.

Solutions to environmental problems involve more than simply recycling and nuclear energy, however. They require new social goals that greatly modify the prodigality of current concepts of social progress, and modify as well the profit motive, the dominance of man over nature and of nations over one another, and commercial and governmental processes.* We cannot go more deeply into this critical subject beyond emphasizing how intimately the intangibles of ethical, social, and cultural considerations are part of the materials, energy, and ecological problems. It is easily demonstrated, however, that here, again, we are dealing with a cybernetic system that includes very many feedback loops, some of which, such as the depletion of resources from waste and expanding gross national product, are bound to reach undesirable ends. But directed toward goals that are conservative, and with negative feedback for control and stability, conditions can be maintained to assure viability for many generations to come.

Food for the multitudes demands very special consideration from the world at large. We do not know how the 3.6 billion individuals of the world can even now be assured the minimum of two thousand calories for daily diet, and the problem worsens every year with more mouths to feed. The food chain is very complex, with considerable interdependence of plants and animals on each other. One

* The interested reader will find these topics discussed at greater length in *Toward a Viable Future for Man*, by the present author (see References).

common although crude representation of both the limitations of food supply and the interdependence of organisms on each other is the following: The photosynthetic process has an efficiency of only about 1%. What are the food requirements for a man who subsists on fish? The food required for producing one pound of man requires, in chain sequence, about ten pounds of bass. These in turn require one hundred pounds of minnows, one thousand pounds of water fleas, and finally ten thousand pounds of algae. Thus the quantity of food required to build higher and higher levels of the food chain is pyramidal. The example also points up the character of the predatory chain that exists in nature, by which each level lives by consuming the organisms of another level.

Some observations on the growth of populations

At the present time the threat of hunger and starvation hangs heavy on millions of inhabitants of the earth. Despite this fearful situation, the increase of population continues at the high rate of 2% each year,* which promises to double the present number of 3.2 billion by the year 2000 and bring a sevenfold increase over the next one hundred years.

The situation brings to the foreground once again the fears expressed by the Englishman Thomas Robert Malthus (1766–1834). In *An Essay on the Principle of Population* (1798), Malthus considered the world's population to be increasing in geometric ratio (1, 2, 4, 8, . . .), while food availability seemed to increase by the much slower arithmetic progression (1, 2, 3, 4, 5, . . .). Nearly every argument advanced by Malthus has been contested and proved to require important qualifications: he did not envision the development of modern industrial capability to produce more food by more-efficient methods or the possibilities of obtaining food from the seas or by synthetic production; nor did he recognize the possibility that as society became technologically more advanced, there would be a reduction of birth rate and a balancing of population against the availability of food. But the facts are: (1) the world's population

---

* A 1% rate of population increase doubles the population in about seventy years. A rate of 2% doubles it in thirty-five years, and a rate of 3% doubles it in twenty-three years. The same considerations apply to economic development and to the national product as an index of progress. Interest payment of 7.2% a year on bank deposits will double the investment in ten years.

has increased fourfold over the 160 years since his pronouncements, (2) most of the world is not technologically advanced at this time, and (3) there are even today occasions when the number of people who are undernourished is comparable to nearly the total world population of his day. Figure 29 illustrates the increase in the population of the world since A.D. 1, and the expected increases up to 2000.

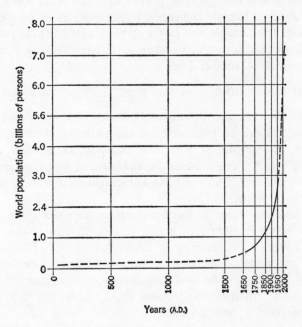

Fig. 29. Estimated population of the world, A.D. 1 to 2000. The solid line represents the portion of the curve about which we have some data.

The assumption that the rate of population increase is determined largely by the availability of food has been proved and disproved many times. In Ireland the introduction of the potato in the late seventeenth century helped to relieve the food problem by increasing the food output per acre. The population also increased from two million to about eight million by 1845. The failure of the crop during that year brought disaster of much larger proportions, when from one to two million died of starvation and as many emigrated.

Since that time, the population has remained about stationary, partly because young people defer marriage to later years.

What are some of the factors that tend to increase breeding rate and population of animals and humans, and what are the influences that stabilize or reduce growth? There seem to be very real differences in the experiences that apply to the non-human world and those that apply to human society. For our purposes, we shall approach the subject through three categories: The first notes the experiences and experiments involving animals. The second involves primitive human societies that depend primarily on collection of wild food rather than on agriculture and technology. The third deals with human societies that utilize agriculture and technology for procurement of food—the more "advanced" societies. Within this last group there are wide differences among nations with respect to the efficiency and effectiveness with which technology aids in the production of food, and some frightening potentialities.

Population controls in non-human societies

The life or death of animal societies is determined partly by the availability of adequate food *per individual animal,* and partly by the effects of hostile weather conditions and predators. There is evidence of natural regulation of numbers in animal societies, which prevents conditions that cause large-scale starvation. For example, studies of the habits of sea birds, which depend on the planktonic organisms that float or grow vertically distended in the North Atlantic Ocean, reveal that as the food supply decreases, the birds distribute themselves over wider areas. The movement is motivated by a search for food but has elements of competition.

Where laboratory experimentation is possible, as with insects, water fleas, guppies, mice, and rats, a pair will breed up to a predictable total number for a particular confinement situation. There is identifiable an apparent maximum (ceiling) population density (number of animals per unit area) for each situation. The number will increase rapidly until this ceiling population density is reached. The number is not likely to go beyond that ceiling density even with abundance of food and complete absence of predators and disease. A three-year series of experiments on guppies gave a remarkable demonstration of regulatory practices that hold numbers to the ceiling density. When guppies were removed at regular intervals, the numbers were soon restored, as more of the young survived. When the stocks were undisturbed, breeding continued at the usual rate, but the excess of numbers was consistently removed by cannibalism at birth.

Regulatory practices vary with each animal society when overpopulation exists. In mice, ovulation and reproduction decline and may even cease; thus population of animals tends to be highly dependent on density, the reproduction rate being great when the population is well below the ceiling density and becoming reduced when the ceiling is reached.

Bird societies resort to a pecking order to establish social hierarchy, to reduce breeding of excessive numbers on the same territory, and to encourage migration. Those that migrate may find other food or become victims of predation or lack of food. In experiments conducted at Aberdeen with Scottish red grouse, it was found that every season produced a population surplus, but the aggressive behavior of dominant males drove away the supernumeraries. The establishing of social hierarchy among animals sometimes tends to maintain a strong and healthy superior group at the expense of the subordinates, keeping the total numbers within acceptable ceiling limits. It is interesting that the processes resulting in population limits tend to become conventionalized. As stated by Wynne-Edwards: "Fighting and bloodshed are superseded by mere threats of violence, and threats in their turn are sublimated into displays of magnificence and virtuosity. This is the world of bluff and status symbols. What takes place, in other words, is a contest for conventional prizes conducted under conventional rules. But the contest itself is no fantasy, for the individual losers can forfeit the chance of posterity and the right to survive."*

It is by such limiting devices that animals maintain some form of equilibrium between their numbers and environmental resources: sometimes by operation of an aggressive social priority, sometimes through hormonal changes that seem to be promoted by excessive population density and that react to discourage breeding, and sometimes by cannibalism or inadequate care or desertion of the young. The restraints on increase are automatic adjustments

---

* See Wynne-Edwards, in References.

(feedback) within the society itself to cope with the numerous uncontrollable influences including food shortage, climate, predation, crowding, and disease.

Population increase in human societies

The experiences of primitive societies of *Homo sapiens* differ in some important respects from those of non-human societies. Food is again largely obtained through hunting and gathering, but with some improvement, in that primitive man can cook and enjoy a larger variety of edibles. He knows how to build shelter for protection and to make clothing for warmth. There are few seasonal limitations on breeding. These all tend to encourage an increase in birth rate, which brings about early crowding and early competition for food and privilege. The establishing of a "pecking order" takes violent form in wars, and disease may spread quickly within the tight assemblies of tribes. There develop taboos and conventions that often tend to restrain breeding. Inadequate care of the young, desertion of the young, and even cannibalism are practiced on occasion. Despite these restraints, large numbers suffer from inadequate food supply in both adulthood and childhood. Part of the reason may lie in the long period of development from infancy to adulthood, the effect being to increase the "momentum" or "mass factor." Birth often occurs at a time when the environment favors breeding and multiplication, but conditions may change severely by the time the child has matured. The effect of this delay in feedback is to increase the tendency to overshoot the control point and to induce severe hunting.

Figure 30 is probably representative of the social conditions that prevail at the present time. Here man utilizes agriculture and technology to increase his food supply. The upper portion of the figure shows a general contraction of the food available to each individual as a result of population increase. The reduction is interrupted at two places in the diagram to represent expansion of available food supply as a result of invention and new technology. It appears that a boost of food supply also often encourages a boost in the birth rate, at least in the early stages of organized society. There also tends to be a boosting of the birth rate due to control of disease, to improvement of environment to

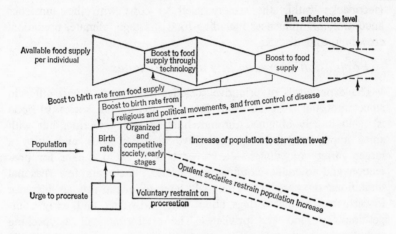

Fig. 30. Population trends among societies that produce food through agriculture. The total food production increases periodically through improved technology, but not enough to keep up with population increases. In many social groups the increase of food supply, successful treatment of disease, and religious and political influences, all tend to increase population to the point of risking periodic starvation. Although the more opulent societies develop voluntary restraints on the birth rate, there persists an over-all threat of overpopulation and large-scale starvation in the world. (From *Introduction to Natural Science*. Courtesy of Academic Press)

assure greater safety and longevity, to political influences, and to religious influences that place sanctity on numbers and on all useful "creations of God."

The lower part of the diagram shows a branching in two general directions as the mass of humanity expands in numbers. One portion finds that the comforts of an opulent society can be achieved and retained only by restricting the size of the family. This portion exercises voluntary restraint to hold down the birth rate, and thus continues with an abundance of food available to its members. There is thereby achieved an equilibrium between population level and food supply. Oddly enough, it is usually the cultures that are highly advanced in technology, and therefore capable of greatly increasing their production of food, that tend to exercise this restraint on population. In societies such as those in the United States, the food needs of the entire population can be provided by engaging only a fraction of the population in agriculture. The severer problem is indicated by the portion of the diagram showing continuously increasing populations, and where in contrast with conditions affecting primitive societies, competition is tempered by humanitarian and religious restraints (except when there is resort to war). Even education is likely to promote awareness only of short-range goals, without looking to the risks of starvation in the more distant future. Every humanitarian effort to increase food supply, reduce disease, improve conditions for healthy birth, assure healthy growth, protect each individual from harm, and assure a long life, seems to work in the direction of promoting a greater calamity in the future.

What are the alternatives? Clearly the restraints to be cultivated do not lie in the practices of the animal world to prevent overpopulation. Just as clearly, the masses of people must be helped to advance beyond the present, intermediate stage of culture and self-control toward effective and humane restraints on population increase.

Nor is the problem of population control without moral and teleological uncertainties. Whether one regards nature with cold, "scientific" analysis, or finds excitement in its immense variety, its awe-inspiring upheavals, its order, its push for life and yet more life, the question of man's existence is unavoidable. The reply of earlier generations, which avoided more than answered the question (man and nature exist for the glory of God), is no longer sufficiently complete or satisfying; and yet no other answer has supplanted it.

Throughout the long history of life on earth there must have been many occasions when a species failed, or nearly failed, to survive for lack of mutually acceptable adjustment to its environment. It appears, however, that never before could a species have foreseen its doom, as can man, in the face of uncompromising demands of ecological balances and the insatiable demands of his own society.

CHAPTER 10

Cybernetics and the Processes of Nature

> Which is the more philosophically challenging aspect of nature, the Second Law of Thermodynamics that predicts ultimate disorder and degradation of energy, or the defiance of that law, if only for a moment, by every blade of grass and every living thing?

From body organs and socioeconomic systems we pass to the more fundamental, evolutionary processes of the biosphere. The functional elements of cybernetic systems will be identifiable in this new context also, but with very interesting variations. For example, every control system is designed to serve a *purpose,* as seen in a system designed to hold constant the temperature of a room. But what can we say to be the "purpose" of the world of living things? We know also that the design or organization of a system incorporates *information,* and that the element of *time* enters its every function. How are we to approach natural processes that incorporate information of increasing complexity through evolutionary processes involving billions of years? Is there indeed something of a "purpose" represented by the transition from microbes to man? And how are we to account for the even larger jump from lifeless inorganic molecules to the first organism that was "alive"? Do the concepts of cybernetics offer any clues to the origin of life?

This last question especially concerns us in this chapter, as does the quotation that begins the chapter. Our approach will be to call into service some of the physical laws that describe natural processes, such as the laws of thermodynamics, and a few details of atomic and molecular structure. Then after noting the physical conditions that existed in the early history of the earth we shall examine the possibilities they offered within a "cybernetic system." The exploration will not give answers to the secrets of nature, but the search nevertheless brings other rewards.

Why we are interested in the second law of thermodynamics

The first and second laws of thermodynamics, which were introduced in Chapter 3, and the introduction to information theory of Chapter 7, will have especial importance for discussing the origin of life. Our interest in the second law, and especially in the entropy (or order/disorder) concept, arises from two exciting situations that involve life on earth. We noted in Chapter 3 that the flow of energy between the various regions of the universe tends to bring all the parts into temperature equilibrium with each other. (Our simple example was the cup of hot coffee losing its heat and assuming the temperature of its environment.) In the process, although the total energy content of the system remains constant, the reduction in *net* energy flow from one object to another makes the energy less and less useful. In other words, the equilibrium state is made up of disordered, useless molecular movements, like a huge army in which every soldier goes his own separate way. Moreover we noted that the move toward disorder is the "highly probable" direction of change, as compared with disorganized things becoming organized.

We associated the concept of *entropy increase* with this trend toward disorder; that is, the entropy is higher for states that have a higher probability of occurrence. Therefore the universal trend seems to be to maximize this characteristic to which we give the name entropy. But then we noted that there is a rather remarkable deviation from the general trend: As energy received from the sun is absorbed or radiated in a thousand different ways toward randomness, a small portion of that energy flows through subtle pathways involving *living organisms*. The pathway involves the energy of sunlight, the photosynthetic process that produces plant substance, and all the living organisms that feed on plants or on each other.

The process involves collecting randomly scattered molecules of carbon dioxide, water, and nitrogenous molecules to form highly organized plant molecules; or consuming molecular aggregates to produce organisms that have ever-more-complex structural and functional properties, represented by the roughly three million species of plant and animal life. Within each organism the entropy change is a decrease, but of course the over-all trend is still an increase when one takes into account the total energy of the sun-and-earth system. It is exciting, nevertheless, that within a universe that seems to be "running down," there exist segments that move in the reverse direction. It is this contrast, which on the surface at least represents a competitive process, that motivates the question that begins the chapter.

Let us compare, as did the physicist Erwin Schrödinger, the behavior of inanimate and of living systems. There is a similarity in that both non-living and living systems are made up of atoms and molecules that are in rapid motion. When left alone, an inanimate system runs down fairly quickly, with gross mechanical or electrical motion coming to a standstill and the molecules taking on the disordered movements of thermodynamic equilibrium, which has been associated with increase in the entropy of the system. In contrast, Schrödinger observed, a living organism is always "doing something" to keep alive, to obtain nourishment from its environment, to delay its own degeneracy as much as possible. Through the processes called metabolism, the body fights decay and in fact increases the degree of its own organization. Schrödinger suggested, "What an organism feeds on is negative entropy."* Why the organism must be "doing something" is not evident. How it does what it does is determined by the *informational elements* stored within the organism, which leads to the second reason for our interest in the second law of thermodynamics.

Entropy, information, and the drive for life

We say that the increase of entropy corresponds to changes in nature toward a "more probable" state. In Chapter 7 we also indicated that the easier it is (more likely or probable) to guess a piece of information, the less value or novelty it contains as information. Thus both the concept of entropy and the concept of information content involve probability considerations. The equation

---

* The term *negentropy* was proposed by L. Brillouin as a contraction of "negative entropy." See References.

for the informational content of a message includes a logarithmic relationship to probability functions, as does the equation for entropy. Is there, therefore, some basic relationship between entropy and information? The answer is in the affirmative. Let us attempt to reason through their relationship without equations:

We can say immediately that an organism has its particular structure and functions by virtue of the information stored in its genetic mechanisms, and that the more complex the organism the more the information that is required to achieve its structure. Also the more complex the organism the lower is the entropy represented by its local state. Therefore *organization, and reduction of entropy, both require the use of information.* Moreover, only when there is available suitable genetic information is it possible to direct efforts and molecules in a direction away from general disorder toward order. Thus the very improbable pathway whereby energy flows through living organisms (on the way to ultimate disorder) is made possible only by virtue of the existence of information to guide it through improbable steps and pathways.

How is the information itself developed? At considerable cost in energy. As Brillouin states it: "Information gain means an increase in the entropy in the laboratory." When one conducts an experiment that reveals some new information, there is considerable use of energy and an over-all increase of entropy in the system of experimenter and experiment. But that same new information can now be publicized and utilized by many other people (or incorporated in the genes of an organism) without expenditure of energy on their part that in any way compares with the energy used in the original experimental processes. In fact it is possible to utilize that information in such a way as to *reduce* the entropy *within a subsystem.*

Each molecular form having definite organization of atoms to give the assembly its molecular characteristics represents incorporation of a certain amount of information in the assembly. According to Quastler,* there is about the same informational content in an amino acid as in a word of a language, while the informational content of a protein molecule might correspond to that contained in a paragraph of prose. The DNA molecule of a mammalian cell,

* See References.

on the other hand, represents a massive assembly amounting to 2×10^{10} bits of information, which has been compared to one hundred sets of the *Encyclopaedia Britannica.* The informational content of the DNA molecule of the bacterium *Escherichia coli,* on the other hand, amounts to about 10^7 bits.

There has been some quantitative comparison of the amount of information required to completely describe the organization of an organism and the amount of heat energy contained in the organism as determined by calorimetric measurements. For example, for the same *E. coli* bacterium, H. J. Morowitz* determined that 2×10^{11} bits of information were required to describe the atomic configuration of the organism in three dimensions, and this seemed to be about what calorimetric measurements revealed to be the energy content of the organism.

But, asks H. A. Johnson,† why the difference between 2×10^{11} bits and 10^7 bits of the DNA of *E. coli?* Why does this bacterium contain about twenty thousand times more information in its structure than is prescribed by the information contained in its DNA molecule? It is in this connection that Johnson sees the need to distinguish between quantity of information and quality of information. In a beautiful analogy he pictures an assembly of eight copies of Euclid's *Elements,* and notes first that the significance of the volumes lies in their content of words, not in the quality of the binding or format of the books, which he characterizes as "purposeless" in relation to informational content of the volumes. Moreover, there is a redundancy in having seven copies additional to any one copy. Even within the one copy there can be a basic distinction between the early pages, which contain thirty-five definitions, five postulates, and ten axioms, and the remaining portions, which contain proofs of nearly five hundred propositions. The latter he would categorize as *derivative information.* The definitions and axioms represent the truly significant and original information of the entire assembly of eight copies—the "purposeful" information.

Johnson goes further by questioning why it is that information theory has been of limited usefulness for making quantitative analyses of biological systems, as compared with its usefulness for ap-

* *Bulletin of Mathematical Biophysics,* 17, 81 (1955).
† Horton A. Johnson, in an article titled "Information Theory in Biology After 18 Years," *Science* 168, 1545 (26 June 1970).

plications in the telecommunications field, for which it was originally proposed. He finds a clue to the weakness in the failure to distinguish between information that is original or "purposeful," and information that is derivative or redundant or downright trivial. Thus while for ordinary electromechanical transmission of signals the primary and exclusive interests are the *quantity* and the *distinguishability* of the signals above noise levels, when considering informational content in biological applications the *quality* features become important as well. That is, the information bits that go to make up an assembly of parts may total vast numbers without there being anything resembling the quality of life in the assembly. The kind of informational storage that makes for life and for living processes he regards to be "purposeful information" of a very special kind. How special it is may perhaps be indicated by the difference between the 2×10^{11} bits of information required to describe the full *E. coli* organism and the 10^7 bits encompassed in its DNA molecule. That is, only one out of twenty thousand bits was truly "purposive" in giving to the bacterium its organizational and functional properties.

Going back to the relationship between information content and negentropy, there is a need to include something besides absence of randomness in the negentropy concept when it applies to a living organism. When discussing entropy change in connection with nonliving energy processes, there is involved both a condition external to the object or phenomenon involved (energy added or subtracted) and an intrinsic, or as Johnson states it, *intensive,* factor represented say by the "temperature" of the object or phenomenon. It is the absence of a quality to compare with this intensive quality that poses an obstacle to more-penetrating understanding of biological processes. For the moment the term "purposeful" information suggested by Johnson may have to serve as a substitute.

We know little about the energy-consuming processes that developed the "information" now incorporated in the DNA and RNA molecules. The "information" now there, however, can be put to work to *organize* random molecules into amino acids, protein molecules, organs, and control systems that include both negative and positive feedback elements, into a "machine" we call a living organism. Schrödinger would say that the living organism maintains its high degree of orderliness (that is, the life processes) by "extracting order from the environment." There is also a reverse process, a breaking down of molecules that goes on at roughly the same rate during the greater part of the life of the organism.

A little on the covalent bond

Before pursuing the question of how life may have emerged, it will be useful to note some of the selection rules that determine how atoms join together. For certainly the existence of "preferences" in chemical combinations would greatly influence the formation of the large protein molecules that make up living matter.

The atomic elements that make up living organisms are carbon, oxygen, hydrogen, nitrogen, and a scattering of other atoms. On inquiring how two oxygen atoms join to form the oxygen molecule, or one oxygen atom combines with two hydrogen atoms to form the water molecule, or a carbon atom combines with two oxygen atoms to form carbon dioxide, etc., we discover some remarkable rules that "govern" molecular assemblies. We recall that every atom has a nucleus made up of positively charged protons and of neutrons, and that each nucleus attracts into its orbit of influence the number of negative electrons required to make the atom electrically neutral. Rather unexpectedly, the attracted electrons do not plunge into the nucleus but retain identity as electrons in some kind of motion around the nucleus. We say that each nucleus and its associated electrons persist in dynamic but stable *energy states,* there being a number of characteristic normal or "excited" energy states for each atom type. Even when severely disturbed, as when an electron is knocked out of its place, the atom will try to find another electron and assume the identical role and energy state that existed with the former electron.

There are other surprises. When analyzing the energy states of atoms it appears that electrons are organized in orbital structures that for lack of a better concept we refer to as "shells." Each shell accommodates only a particular number of electrons. When the shell is full, as in the case of the helium atom (with two electrons) or the neon atom (with ten electrons), the atom is found to be especially stable and non-reactive with other atoms. When a shell lacks an electron, or when there is just one more electron than a full shell, the atom is highly reactive toward other atoms. Therefore fluorine and chlorine, the shells of which are one electron short of being full, are highly reactive, while lithium and sodium are also highly reactive because they have each just one electron in excess of full shells.

Thus it is that even though an atom is neutral with respect to balancing positive and negative charges, its *reactivity* (or lack of reactivity) *toward other atoms is determined very strongly by the degree of completeness of its electronic shell structure.* It will, in fact, join with another atom in such a way that each of the pair of atoms *simulates* a complete shell. For example, the hydrogen atom has a positive proton for a nucleus and a single negative electron and is quite reactive because the smallest shell accommodates two electrons when full; but when two hydrogen atoms combine they share each other's electrons and thereby simulate full shells for each without disturbing the electrical neutrality. The bonding of atoms by this sharing of electrons is called *covalent bonding.* It is important also to note that it is an unusual form of asymmetry in the individual atoms that brings about the combination.

Many atoms join through covalent bonds, among the most interesting being combinations that involve the carbon atom. Carbon, with six electrons, lacks four electrons of having a full shell of ten corresponding to the stable neon atom. Because it is missing so many, it is not at all as reactive toward other atoms as is oxygen, which lacks two electrons. Nevertheless the carbon atom also joins with other atoms to complete its shell. It can join with four hydrogen atoms to form methane (CH_4) or still another carbon and six hydrogens to form ethane (C_2H_6). And so the chain may grow until a single large protein molecule may contain many hundreds of carbon atoms in various chain formations, many oxygen and hydrogen atoms, and here and there nitrogen atoms, all because each atom attempts to simulate closed shells. This is the reason for the statement that perhaps when we understand the *why* of the covalent bond of atoms we shall also have some inkling of the "purposes" of life and of nature itself.

There are other forms of attraction as well, due largely to asymmetries in electric charge that may exist on atoms or on parts of large molecules. (According to Coulomb's law for electric charges, unlike charges attract each other while like charges repel each other.) These asymmetries of charge form weak or strong bonds between molecule parts, referred to as hydrogen bonds and as Van der Waals attractive forces. At any rate, it appears that influences governing the bonding of atoms to each other have much to do with giving *direction* to the patterns that molecular assemblies may assume. We shall return to this presently.

On parts and wholes and machine organization

We have indicated how closely the characteristics of a system are determined by the organizational and functional relationships of its parts to each other. Systems may have many parts. The wheel of a bicycle, for example, has many interesting design features. However, it is only when a rider takes advantage of the structural and functional features of the wheel (that is, joins with the wheel) that there emerges the totally new function of riding the bicycle. The human body is made up largely of water molecules and about twenty kinds of amino-acid molecules, but by no stretch of the imagination could one envision their individual properties to be the basis for the living, walking, talking, thinking, and reproduction functions that emerge in the form of man.

It will be useful to consider these principles in terms of a *machine*. As defined by Ashby,* "A 'machine' is that which behaves in a machine-like way, namely, that its internal state, and the state of its surroundings, defines uniquely the next state it will go to." The machine concept does not require materiality in the construction of the "machine" or energy considerations for its operation, the requirement being only that it perform with regularity in a "law-abiding" and "machine-like" way. The concept as defined therefore permits biological as well as mechanical systems to be thought of in terms of a machine. There comes next the question of the "purposes" of the machine and whether it is properly organized to function in a manner that satisfies those purposes. There are "good" organizations, "bad" organizations, and sometimes possibilities for changing the organization of the machine to meet its purposes; and whether the organization is good or bad at any instant of time depends on the performance required at each instant of time and under each condition of environmental change. The machine that is guided too much by memory of past experiences may have diffi-

---

* W. Ross Ashby, "Principles of the Self-Organizing System," in *Principles of Self-Organization*, edited by H. von Foerster and George W. Zopf (New York: Pergamon Press, 1962). The article is also reproduced in the book edited by Buckley, in References.

culty in meeting new situations satisfactorily, since its actions are largely habit-determined. (Ashby's example is a rat that has become accustomed to good food and thereby readily accepts poisoned food without suspicion.) Also, the degree of organization of a living organism must be suited to the degree of organization (or disorganization) of the terrestrial environment in which it lives. Should an environment require the organism to change, the organism must be capable of reorganizing itself to continue to perform satisfactorily.

The ability to reorganize to meet new situations usually requires capability on the part of the machine to establish new interconnections among its parts, as when the separated nerve cells in the embryo begin to grow dendrites and synaptic interconnections. The machine would thereby be "self-organizing," and the reorganization would be considered "good" if, for example, the feedback influences were eventually to become negative and reasonably stabilizing versus positive and destructive. (Ashby gives the example of a fire-seeking child developing new thinking capabilities that make it fire-avoiding.) But then, Ashby argues, no machine can be organizing of itself alone; it may achieve this capability only when to that machine there is coupled another machine. We would add that even the addition of other machines would do little good unless there is also a purpose, or goal orientation, or goal-seeking element in the system, as well as addition of information that makes possible new functional capabilities.

The idea that machines are self-organizing is not a good one, in Ashby's opinion. Rather, it is better to conceive that *"every isolated determinate dynamic system obeying unchanging laws will develop 'organisms' that are adapted to their 'environments.'"* The reason is that systems in general tend toward states that are in equilibrium with their environment. One way to view this is that the system is perpetually changing until and except when it is in some form of equilibrium with its environment. Whitehead notes that animals also adapt the environment to their needs in the form of nests, dammed rivers, etc., while in the case of man ". . . this active attack on the environment is the most prominent fact of his existence." The end products or "states" achieved during this move are determined by the preferences that are "favored." (We might assume that the preferred chemical combinations that were discussed earlier are aspects of this "preferred" direction.) When the total system with which we begin is sufficiently complex, as in the case of the primitive earth system, the end results of this move toward equilibrium states may end up as a host of organisms or "machines," each of which is in reasonably stable equilibrium with its terrestrial environment. Thus each animal or plant organism achieves a state of equilibrium by deriving energy and nutrition, reproducing its own kind, and making reasonable adjustment to its neighbors and to its physical environment. But all this becomes possible only as *information* is available and is utilized to an extent commensurate with the complexity of the over-all system.

The primitive earth system

Along with these physical laws and ideas, it will be useful to identify some of the conditions that may have existed on earth before the emergence of life. We picture the hot rays of the sun beating down, and the land and briny waters seething with the heat of the day and the cold of the night. This was about the time when gravitational attraction is thought to have heated the interior of the earth and caused the earth to spew out gases to form the atmosphere over new surfaces of land and water. The atmosphere was probably made up largely of hydrogen (H_2), methane (CH_4), and ammonia (NH_3), quite unlike our present atmosphere of roughly 78% nitrogen (N_2) and 21% oxygen (O_2).

What may we imagine to have been the earth processes of the time? We can guess that at least the following conditions existed:

1. There was certainly an abundance of energy and commotion in this system. The surface and atmosphere as well as the interior of the earth probably experienced much more turbulent motion and interaction than we witness in our own day. This suggests that there was a much higher probability for one part of the earth to interact with another part, and that conditions of pressure, temperature, and combinations of atoms were probably much more varied and intense than those we now witness.

2. There was present in this maelstrom a factor that gradually lost its significance until there came the recent threats of annihilation by nuclear bombs. This was the presence of intense ionizing radiations emitted from radioactive atoms in the earth. It is possible that the ionizing radiations that reached the earth from cosmic processes

in outer space were also of substantially higher levels than they are now.

3. It is not unreasonable to assume that the "laws" governing bonding of atoms to each other were the same as those that we recognize in our own day. But while the same preferential laws of combination existed, we can assume that the more intense environmental conditions under which interactions could take place were conducive to producing both associative and dissociative reactions that are not as often observed at the present time.

For example, intense rays of ionizing radiation induce reactions that may be significantly different from those observed in other situations. The energy that is concentrated along the ionization track of a fast alpha particle can be many thousand times greater than can be concentrated by any other means. Lightning discharges, which we can assume to have been prevalent and intense, could have been important in the formation of new situations and new compounds. These, then, went to constitute the parts or elements of our earth system and the conditions under which the parts existed.

4. There were *continuously changing interrelationships* between the parts and their environments, the "parts" being sometimes a few molecules and sometimes vast bodies of matter transported from one region to another. We might attempt an analogy in the anthropomorphic terms of a man and a maiden: Just as the relationship between a young man and a young woman is determined in part by their own personal inclinations and in part by the social, cultural, and physical environments in which they meet, so it is with atoms. Note, however, that each young man and young woman form part of the environment of other young men and women. There is therefore a circularity, or feedback, influence one on the other: every change affecting a particular young man and woman becomes a change in the environment of other, neighboring young men and women.

As an example, suppose that we begin with a system that includes carbon, oxygen, and hydrogen atoms and methane (CH_4) molecules. The interactions that can take place are limited to these compounds. If for the moment we think of carbon and hydrogen as the central figures and the remainder as their environment, we can suppose that in the course of time, conditions become right for carbon and hydrogen to join a methane molecule to produce a new compound, namely the ethane molecule (C_2H_6). The event represents more than just the production of a new compound, for the environment of all the other atoms and molecules will have changed by the addition of ethane. Also, now other carbon and hydrogen atoms can join with ethane to produce propane (C_3H_8). And thus the chain can take on the growth properties of a *system with positive feedback* for the production of larger and larger molecules.

5. There is another feature that may enter when the environment includes a variety of compounds and new conditions. This has to do with some of the compounds acting as *catalysts* to produce reactions between other atoms, sometimes simply by their presence as "third bodies." For example, when hydrogen and oxygen react, they do so explosively, with emission of a great deal of heat energy. However, the two gases can be mixed and remain completely non-reactive at ordinary temperatures until a spark initiates the reaction or until platinum is introduced to catalyze the reaction. The catalyst is not itself consumed by the process. In quite another manner, the metabolic processes of living organisms would not take place at all at body temperatures were it not for the participation of vast numbers of proteins called *enzymes,* which serve as catalysts.

A look at molecular movements

While we are on the subject of interaction tendencies of atoms, it will be interesting to look at some of their physical movements as well. We noted that a single cubic centimeter of air contains over 10^{19} molecules, all in random motion and in collision with one another. The number of collisions that take place each second is enormously large. If in a container of gas or liquid we were to place a perforated diaphragm (Fig. 31), the molecules would collide and

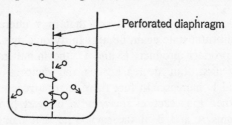

Fig. 31. Molecules move through the perforations with great speed and frequency, thereby keeping the concentration essentially the same on the two sides.

move in and out of the holes of the diaphragm and keep the concentration of molecules on the two sides essentially the same. (The term *essentially* is necessary because at any instant of time there could be many thousands more molecules in one cubic centimeter than in other areas of equal volume, but this difference is still small in terms of percentages and likely to change too rapidly for any instrument to measure.)

Now, if in a small container or test tube (Fig. 32) we place not

Fig. 32. In a small test tube, atom types A and B react to produce products C and D, and easily reach an equilibrium state in which there are as many decompositions of C and D to return A and B to the solution as there are interactions of A and B to produce C and D.

just one molecule type but two types that may interact with each other, an equilibrium state again obtains fairly quickly: Atoms A and B interact to produce products C and D, the initial interaction rate being high at first, but decreasing as the concentrations of the products C and D increase. In fact there is soon reached an equilibrium point, when the reaction *reverses* to convert products C and D back to atoms A and B at the same rate that new products are formed. Equilibrium states therefore represent balances of forward and reverse processes involving statistical averages of collisions and interactions. In a small test tube the interactions are very rapid, unobtrusive, and quickly sensitive to the concentrations of the reactants. The reaction is equally swift and unobtrusive on the cellular scale in the body.

But now let us take the same atom types A and B in large volume, and design a reaction system that resembles the conventional tanks, towers, and pipes of a petroleum refinery (Fig. 33). The inputs of

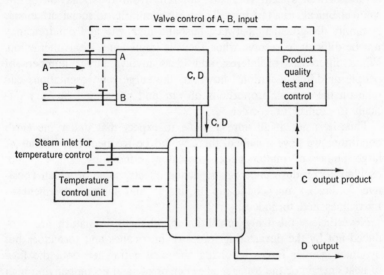

Fig. 33. In a large reactor vessel, the input and output of the system are separated from each other, and controls are required to regulate temperatures, pressures, input rates for A and B, and the output rates and quality of products C and D.

A and B must usually be controlled, the rates being determined by the quality of products C and D or by other considerations. Other variables must also be controlled, such as the temperature and pressure of the tank in which the products accumulate before they flow out separately. Errors in temperature may, for example, prevent complete separation of C and D into the two outgoing streams. In fact, as every control engineer knows, great care must be taken to prevent the occurrence of oscillations, vibrations, surges of change in product quality and product flow, and general misbehavior of the system, which sometimes can lead to destruction of the system itself.

The larger volumes, delays in flow of heat, and delays in response of instruments, all contribute to make control uncertain. There can easily develop positive feedback, which accentuates surges and produces oscillations or self-destructive tendencies that are difficult to control.

Whatever the process, it is clear that with larger dimensions the behavior of a system is vastly different from the behavior of the same chemicals in a test tube. There is a similarity to social situations: A family disagreement between husband and wife and children may not be difficult to resolve when there is immediate, local interaction. When differences of interest and ideas involve larger numbers of people or different nations, however, the surges and oscillations can take on the serious proportions of war and peace and be very difficult to control or correct.

Thus it is not at all unreasonable to expect that under the earth conditions we have assumed, there would be frequent interactions of large bodies of matter under oscillatory conditions. Once begun, oscillations produce uncertain feedback effects, some of which (positive feedback) may build up to larger and larger movements— hurricanes and tornadoes.

Nevertheless the truly revolutionary changes in nature are produced not by the devastating forces of hurricanes and tornadoes but by much gentler forces involving chemical action, erosion, the flow of heat energy, or the transfer of water or of sand accompanying high tide and low tide. For example, very unusual patterns of ripples, crests, and troughs develop when a pebble is dropped in a quiet pool of water. The patterns become especially complex when there are two or more points of disturbance that produce interacting traveling waves.

A hundred years ago the philosopher Herbert Spencer in his book *First Principles* (1867 edition) saw great significance in the changes that develop when a simple mixture of shellac dissolved in petroleum is allowed to evaporate: As the evaporation proceeds to dryness the shellac takes on a remarkable honeycomb structure, the effect being interpreted as due to the viscous forces and surface forces. Spencer interpreted these results as illustrating the very essence or fundamental characteristics of evolutionary processes in nature, namely transition from homogeneous structure to non-homogeneous structure. Moreover, the more non-homogeneous a structure, the larger the number of parameters that are required to describe the structure.

Thus Spencer associated the evolution of structure with the presence of flow conditions, and postulated their existence even within inanimate materials. The concept was extended when at the turn of the century the French scientist H. Bénard demonstrated the transitions that take place when a flat plate containing a liquid is heated slowly and uniformly. At a given critical temperature the homogeneous transparent liquid begins to develop a structure. Rings resembling cylindrical tubes begin at the edge and move inward to fill the entire vessel with a honeycomblike structure. It was Lord Rayleigh who sixteen years later explained the phenomenon to be due to the interaction of two flow conditions, namely the flow of heat energy upward and the downward flow of the cooler surface liquid: "The layer rapidly resolves itself into a number of *cells,* the motion being an ascension in the middle of a cell and a descension at the common boundary between a cell and its neighbors." There are two phases, the first being relatively short (one to two seconds for less-viscous liquids such as alcohol or benzene, ten seconds for paraffin, several minutes for viscous oils).* Neither flow is in any sense near the equilibrium state, but their interaction creates an especially unstable situation that produces the honeycomb structure. The second phase approaches a permanent regime of regular hexagons, until it disappears with further heating.

It should be noted that the structure that develops is not only a structure in space, but a structure in time in that the structure disappears with time. Moreover, the entire process requires a continuous input of energy, as in life processes, and the structure quickly disappears when energy input ceases. In fact, one may visualize the process of a structure development and disappearance as alternating —having the characteristics of oscillating systems.

Indeed cyclic processes are common in living systems, and they exhibit a wide variety of periods. There is the inhalation and exhalation of air many times each minute, the intake of food several times each day, and the daily excretion of wastes. There is the cycle

---

* *Philosophical Magazine* Vol. XXXII, pp. 529–46, or in *Scientific Papers by Lord Rayleigh,* Vol. VI, pp. 432–46 (New York: Dover Publications Inc., 1964). I am indebted to a lecture given by Aharon Katchalsky of Israel for recalling this example.

of sleep and wakefulness. Over all, there is the cycle of birth and of death, which returns the body to the earth. Each aspect requires a dissipative form of "equilibrium" involving energy exchange with the environment. Each has aspects that resemble the control of large chemical plants.

Some of these conditions can be duplicated in the laboratory, and indeed the "hot, soupy" conditions that have been postulated for early earth conditions have been simulated with remarkable results. Many of the organic molecules that are components of living tissue, such as amino acids, sugars, polyphosphates, pyrimidines, and purines have been produced in the laboratory.

With these in mind Aharon Katchalsky would observe that life is not a product of probabilistic phenomena, but the result of powerful flows interacting under conditions that are far from equilibrium, or an open system that is far from equilibrium and involves a dissipative flow of energy that combines to give a four-dimensional spatio-temporal structure. The structure of life has a narrow range of existence, and when shifted out of this narrow range the structure disappears and death ensues. From this we proceed to ideas that are even more speculative.

On the formation of biological agglomerates

Dynamic conditions in the physical world are more likely to break down molecular assemblies into their parts than to form larger structures. Rocks are crushed by their own interaction to become the sand of the shore. Flowing water erodes rocks and reduces mountains. Ionizing radiation usually breaks molecular bonds. There are, nevertheless, abundant opportunities for sediments to slowly form large beds of solid rock and large crystalline formations. And in some quieter nook there can be many occasions for scattered fragments to come together and form new relationships. Even ionizing radiation can under certain conditions promote the cross-linking of molecules to form new, larger molecules (polymerization). Indeed it is this last effect that has given new scope to the plastics industries. Let us theorize one possible sequence of changes involving these compounds. We begin with conditions ("soupy," colloidal), from which there may evolve larger and larger macromolecules and agglomerates that preceded and made possible the emergence of life.

1. We shall note again that *asymmetries* in charge distribution tend to give parts of a molecule slightly positive or slightly negative electric-charge characteristics. The slightly negative portions of one molecule will then be attracted to the slightly positive portions of another molecule to form a much larger molecule or to give the molecules and the solution a semicrystalline, ordered array. Water molecules can form such ordered array, for example.

2. There have been notable successes in producing biochemical compounds (i.e., compounds that are normally produced within a living organism) by synthetic means. Encouraged by the proposals of A. I. Oparin, Urey in 1952 and Miller in 1953 reported that amino acids, urea, and other organic compounds had been produced in glass apparatus containing methane, ammonia, hydrogen, and water when the mixture was subjected to spark discharge. Using ultraviolet light or other ionizing radiation, experimenters soon produced a variety of amino acids as well as groups of amino acids forming peptides and polypeptides, which are basic structural components of proteins. Additional variations were introduced in the presence of high temperature (Harada and Fox; see Fox in References). Thus the road toward production of proteins appears to have had a start, if *only* a start.

Along another direction, irradiation of adenosine and ethyl metaphosphate with ultraviolet radiation (or irradiation of adenosine, ribose, and phosphoric acid) produced nucleoside adenosine and the various other related compounds such as ADP (adenosine diphosphate) that are so important for energizing biochemical reactions. Still another direction gave the beginnings for the production of nucleotides by the interaction of sugars, bases, and phosphates and the condensation of these nucleotides into long chains of polynucleotides (DNA etc.). But while these and other successes are impressive achievements, they still represent only the very beginning steps toward production of the vast numbers of types of macromolecules that make up the living body.

3. When molecules cling together, it is not unusual for one branch of the new macromolecule to be soluble in water and another branch of the same molecule to be soluble in oil. When such molecules are in a solution that includes water and oil, they form a thin but moderately stable interface, or membrane between the two

fluids.* The membrane may then close in on itself to form cell-like sacs, which may enclose a fluid of different composition from the fluid in which the sac itself floats. Of course there is always present the tendency of water droplets to assume spherical shape. When therefore a liquid mixture contains a variety of macromolecules, water, and fatty substances, there is a tendency for drops to form, called *coacervates,* which in some cases may be large enough to be visible to the naked eye as a composite of sacs, each enclosed in some kind of membrane "structure." At any rate, in solution macromolecules develop suspensions and become gel-like and lose much of their freedom and random motion in favor of some form of *tenuous macrostructure.* The polarized water molecule may especially give the fluid and membranous structures a semicrystalline or highly organized character.

4. Because the bonding energies between the side chains of molecules are relatively weak, they can easily make and break from only moderate changes in temperature, acidity, concentration, or composition. Coacervates may also change structure easily as the environment changes. That is, the tenuous macrostructure alters its form in response to changes in the solution environment. *Sensitivity of structure to internal and to environmental conditions* is one of the key requirements in living organisms, as we shall see.† At this point, sensitivity to environment represents activity that has a highly fluid character; nevertheless the adjective "structured" is applicable.

5. There may come next a stage when the sensitivity of that agglomerate of intertwined molecules develops a more *aggressive and intimate exchange relationship* with its environment. That is, the agglomerate exchanges energy and materials with its environment. The exchange could presumably begin only as a periodic flow of fluid that leaves some residue on its return. As was indicated for chemical and physical systems, reversible reactions and oscillations can develop fairly easily. Moreover, since absolute restoration to initial conditions is a rarity, there is a strong likelihood that a "residue" effect will soon develop.

6. Oscillations, or hunting, represent states of dynamic equilibrium,

---

* These processes are discussed in Chapters 3 and 12 of Part II, "The Life Sciences," of *Introduction to Natural Science* (see References).
† This does not imply that all inorganic substances lack sensitivity of structure to environmental conditions.

the stability of which is presumably maintained by the presence of negative feedback. But even under equilibrium conditions, the structure of the compound we are discussing must continue to be "tenuous" and subject to change.

7. Whatever the nature of changes, a subsystem that was once in equilibrium with its environment must either readjust and adapt to the changes or cease to function. Even while changes are enhanced through positive feedback, it is conceivable that some form of negative feedback can evolve, the net effect being to find and hold new states of dynamic equilibrium. We can expect that this build-up process, as well as the finding of new equilibrium conditions, will be guided by "preferred orientations," which are characteristic of the molecular assemblies. Perhaps genetic mutations can be regarded in this light (Fig. 28).

8. Somewhere along the line there enters the element of *information storage*. Just as the flow of water may leave a path that in time becomes a river bed, so we may picture each new experience or event as increasing the likelihood of there being a repetition of the experience. The process may have the nature of a sieve, which permits only particles smaller than a certain size to pass through, or may involve a selection process according to chemical affinity of atoms and molecules. Or there may be a matching of frequencies of vibration. In any case, "information" might begin as a selectivity or matching phenomenon that leads to repetition, and information storage or memory. We can picture the process as similar to the selection of data presented or retained in a computer in the form of punched cards or magnetized tapes. Or even more pertinent, we know that the information code utilized by living organisms derives simply from the structural order in which the base molecules that make up the DNA molecules are arranged.

9. We seem to have arrived at a critical stage of what might have been the evolutionary processes leading toward the origin of life. Our picture suggests the existence of cell-like coacervates composed of smaller bodies each of which has its own sensitivity or reactivity to changes in the environmental fluid. That is, when the acidity or temperature of the environmental fluid changes, one or more parts of the "cell" may change also. A day-and-night change in lighting or in temperature conditions could then induce a rhythmic reponse in the "cell" behavior as well. We note also that the likelihood exists

that the rhythmic structural change follows a pattern of "information" that is embodied in the structure itself.

The origin of life

We have arrived at a stage of our highly conjectured evolutionary processes when it is necessary to pause and ask what are the fundamental features of the life processes for which we must find explanations. The formation of biomolecules, which has been discussed, is a necessary but far from sufficient condition. Similarly the incorporation of information in the structure of a "cell" or of a protein molecule is necessary but again not an answer as to how that information becomes useful in the production of more cells or proteins of the same kind.

Following a description given by Henry Quastler (see References), we can expect that the molecular parts of macromolecules might form a complementary double macromolecule (much as we currently envisage for the DNA process) that then dissociates into single macromolecules each of which might become an agent for assembling complementary macromolecules. The synthesis and dissociation would certainly not be unfailingly correct; therefore there could be reproduced new varieties of macromolecules. Also under each condition of environmental mix there would be a higher probability for some molecular reactions to demonstrate superior "adaptability" to changes in the environment.

At some point along the way, we theorize, the exchange between the subsystem and the environment may take on patterns that are more involved than can be represented by simple oscillatory movements. It would take only a slightly more complex path, or include a storage area between membranous boundaries, to change the oscillatory or rhythmic behavior of the system very substantially. The reduction in concentration of "raw materials" inside one part of the globule could cause inflow to restore the concentration, providing the membrane barrier is permeable to these molecules. More likely, however, some form of feedback might have to be invoked to induce inflow to make up for the depletion. The globule could then grow in size, and it is not inconceivable that the cycles of day and night might be a major factor in promoting synthesis, dissociation, multiplication of polynucleotides, and thereby the growth of the globule.

Perhaps we are now on the verge of having a *living organism,* for the essential processes of life do indeed demand this form of interchange or transformation of energy. (Note, however, that the distinctions in these particular terms are still hazy and find their counterparts in the behavior of some strictly chemical systems as well.)

The interchange of energy between the living organism and its environment cannot be haphazard if the organism is to survive. The interchange of energy must therefore be controlled—with control systems that include detectors, motor devices, sources of energy, and feedback associated with each of the variables that must be controlled. Indeed at each progressive stage the organism must add a network of controls, each having its own variables and controls but each integrated with the others in such a way as to make possible a high degree of co-ordination. Some controls have the function of preserving "status quo" in as unchanging a manner as possible, while others must permit adaptation to new situations. The latter capability appears to require a combination of negative and positive feedback influences. Indeed the co-ordination of a complex living system requires extensive use of both kinds of functions.

An even more remarkable phenomenon must now come into play that more than any other feature identifies a living system. The phenomenon is the division and *multiplication of cells* that also leads to *production of progeny.* At first glance the process of producing "more of the same" has the appearance of positive feedback at work, but we know that the reproduction processes are guided from beginning to end by genetic information and by negative feedback influences that restrict the process to that coded information. This is probably true even in the case of cancerous growth, wherein the uncontrolled (positive feedback) influences are somewhat more pronounced, at the expense of the integrated, negative feedback. The occurrence of an event representing mutation would, however, still-further enhance the possibilities for departing from the old pattern toward an organism possessing new genetic information and a new set of controls.

At any rate, organisms may grow and multiply to great complexity. Out of this there somehow develops a requirement that each organism join with another of its own kind to produce progeny, the two being "male" and "female." The partners to the reproduction process being alike and yet not identical, exact reproduction becomes meaningless. The process therefore combines the genetic features of each partner but with variations on each that may lead to greater complexity, from which there may come new functions. Truly the functions that accompany the changing organisms and new structures are new and far removed from the agglomerate of intertwined molecules with which we began. Moreover, by this new mating requirement for producing progeny, nature decrees that to the chaotic, random interactions that are possible in natural processes there will be added a more systematic and more dependable process for evolving new organisms. *This, then, establishes the basic processes for biological evolution, the key processes coinciding with the establishment of a unique combination of positive and negative feedback with information storage.* We must emphasize that the new properties emerging from positive feedback are retained only when follow-up with negative feedback retains the emergent changes. Negative feedback, in turn, is dependent on suitable information being incorporated in the "memory" of the system.

The sequence of steps just described has elements of the mechanical approach or conjecture based largely on ignorance, as indeed is the case. The postulated "tenuous macrostructure" and its sophisticated successors are inadequate to explain the structural features of even the simplest of nature's creatures, let alone explain the sensory complex that allows man to transcend his body capabilities and acquire a mind that reaches for understanding of itself and of the universe.

CHAPTER 11

Cybernetics and Sociocultural Relationships

> "In human life, design implies the acceptance and even the deliberate choice of certain constraints which are of the past and of the environment. But design is also the expression of free will because it always involves value judgments and anticipates the future."*
>
> René Dubos

The long evolutionary processes of the biological world do not lead only to refinement of animal or machine-like functions. For within the superb organism called man there emerges yet a second "miracle," to which we give the names *language, thought processes, reason, symbolism,* and *social and cultural values*. These are even less definable and less tangible than are the definitions for the first "miracle," which we call life. They represent both processes and end products in the search for values, for significance, for meaning and relevance to the purposes of nature. They become at once the highest achievement of nature and of man as well as the sorest obstacle to the unity and peace of mankind. They promote fierce competition for gains that are not counted in terms of food, land, or biological needs. Emerging from the long processes of the past without being able to identify either their source, their lineage, or their ultimate goals, the new interests nevertheless reach vigorously into an uncertain future. On occasion they breathe spiritual qualities and visionary hopes that are not at all congruous with the world we touch and feel. It is fitting that the volume should end with an effort to view these aspects also within the framework of cybernetics.

* From "Future-Oriented Science," in *Perspectives in Planning* (Paris: Organization for Economic Co-operation and Development, 1969).

Species and social organizations

The discussions of Chapter 10 gave little assurance that physical processes with which we have familiarity could on their own have brought about the formation of organisms that could receive "the breath of life" or could have promoted growth and dramatic changes until at present there are about three million species varying all the way up to the complex organism we call man.

Whatever the background and history, each of the three million or so species seems to find its own ecological niche and "balance" within its own membership and with other species and populations. At first glance one is tempted to outline an attractive systems representation for this happy state.

On closer examination, however, one soon finds that the "balance" is far from secure. At best, the species survive through forms of cannibalism as part of a complex food chain and web. This reduces the ecological niche of an organism to largely one of eating other organisms until being eaten by another organism or dying from some other cause.

As to the species called man, his biochemical attributes seem only refinements over those of many other animals. His distinction lies in greater mental capabilities, although even here the distinction is perhaps more in degree than in total difference. Just as we felt unsafe in attributing the origin of life strictly to physical laws, we are even more unsafe in attributing the mental capabilities of man altogether to biochemical processes of the kind with which we are familiar. It would be as sensible to emphasize the similarity of computers to wheelbarrows because both are of metal and have wheel-like gadgets, or overstressing similarity of computers to electric light bulbs because both utilize electric energy.

Although early man was not the hardiest of organisms or the strongest of body among living creatures, mental advantages gave him the upper hand in an evolutionary development that was exceedingly rapid. In our own day, among all the creatures on earth it is given to man alone to contemplate the panorama of nature with some appreciation for the magnificence of its detail and historical scope. From this pinnacle only man may question the steps and relationships that led from the beginning to his own time.

There are less-attractive differences, as well, between man's society and animal societies. In the case of plants and animals, every organism derives (or "borrows") its body substance and sustenance directly or indirectly from soil and water and atmosphere, eventually returning everything to the earth in approximately the same natural form. In contrast, man has learned to exploit the earth's inner energy and material resources as well. He builds cities and enormous industrial and commercial enterprises to satisfy the natural and artificial demands of his society. In contrast with the conservative patterns of the plant and animal worlds, however, man's way of life has initiated a non-restoring spiral that contains elements of positive feedback of a persisting kind, which threatens destruction for man and beast alike.

The spiral develops from many influences. There is first the factor of population increase beyond the capacity of the earth to feed. Within the United States even a trillion-dollar economy based on mass production and automation and rooted in an advanced sense of social justice and responsibility, has failed to provide food for all its hungry, or shelter and safety for all the people. The trillion-dollar economy is itself proving to be an unmanageable beast, because in the absence of new concepts of social goals and purposes, the economy must continue to grow beyond the capabilities of the nation to support that growth, or become cause for national depression and recession.

As to natural energy and material resources, the earth's oil and natural gas supplies will be consumed within a matter of decades, and coal within only another couple of centuries. The atmosphere and the waters of the earth are being polluted, some beyond recovery. Extensive and careless use of pesticides, commercial fertilizers, and chemical products have introduced changes in ecosystems the consequences of which are not yet fully appreciated. The impact is world-wide. The United States' trillion-dollar economy will become even more inflationary as the costs for eliminating pollution begin to be felt, especially as the burden of a vast military machine adds to the costs and to the waste.

It will not be easy to discover solutions to this spiraling situation in the form either of new patterns for self-government or of other strong negative feedback. Experimentation goes on under the banners of capitalism, socialism, communism, and other "isms" to find new forms of government and self-government that meet current needs more effectively, thus far without too much success. Nor is the experimentation confined to governments, for this is a period of history when the thinking man is more than ever puzzled about his own individual role. Theories of government and jurisprudence vary from one extreme to another. The general trend seems to be toward submerging individual goals, responsibility, and self-discipline within a larger system wherein the feedback and controls are mass-controlled (not to say mob-controlled).

Mechanical and social systems compared

The earlier discussions of cybernetic systems minimized distinctions between physical, biological, and social situations. For example, concepts associated with the terms "computer" and "machine" were as useful when dealing with one type of situation as with another. This was proper to do, and the flexibility will be retained in this chapter as well. But while in a chemical or electromechanical process the input of reactants and energy produces material products or some form of interaction with the environment, in the animal body the outputs of muscle activity, biological growth, and waste products are accompanied by unique behavioral and mental activities as well. The physical evidences of movement, anger, love, are accompanied by intangibles in the form of memory, ideas, changed values, or new mental interrelationships. And while any cybernetic system is considered to be goal-oriented or "purposeful," there are likely to be rather major differences in the purposes designed into electromechanical systems as opposed to those found in living organisms.

We have stated that every control system includes variables, transform devices, sensors/detectors, motor devices, energy sources, feedback, and the elements of purpose and of "information." There are vast differences, however, between the information that is processed in the form of electric pulses in an electromechanical system, and communication between two individuals whose sensory processes also utilize electric pulses.

Language, speech, and writing are notoriously inadequate for fully expressing the ideas that a person may wish to communicate to another person. To make matters worse, the receiver of the faulty communication adds his own interpretations based on differing personalities, differing educational and cultural background, differing geographic conditions, differing current mood and environment, and differences due to being hungry or overfed. Even at the professional level each discipline develops its own special terms and lingo. When the number of languages and the confusion are multiplied by many hundreds there evolves the condition we actually have in human societies, for which the nearest analogy recalls the city and tower of Babel.

These all contribute toward creating vast differences in social systems with respect to purposes and goals. The differences we said existed between parents and children become magnified as one proceeds outward from the family into the realm of local physicians, attorneys, storekeepers, builders, police stations, jailhouses, government offices, and become almost impossibly different as one moves into foreign countries. The varieties one finds in cultural, religious, governmental, and social situations are both the sources of enrichment of human existence and the sources of endless misunderstandings and conflicts. Moreover, in the economic and technological realms there are extremes of "progress" and lack of progress, and of wealth and poverty, extremes being found within the borders of almost any nation and becoming especially pronounced between the "have" and "have not" nations and societies. Within this century governmental patterns, objectives, and methods seem to have taken diverse routes that make common effort and co-operation even more difficult because of intent to utilize communication techniques to promote misunderstanding and disunity rather than to promote co-operation between nations. And the ideas, symbols, and concepts that emerge from all this may on occasion become so overpowering as to reduce every other biological interest to subservience, even at the cost of life itself.

Signals, symbols, and idols

The neurological control processes of the body represent cybernetic systems that are directed by sensory signals or by stored genetic code information. There is in man, however, a feature that is difficult to embody in the machine concept even when that machine embodies the most complex of computer capabilities. This has to do with the sense of judgment and of values, of reason, of identity and purpose, of time, of exploration and creativity that go beyond the world of signals into a world of *symbols*.

It represents both a product of, and *transcendence beyond,* man's other capabilities. It is the basis for man's sociocultural development through abstract ideas and language. It is the door to self-awareness, with a past, a present, and a future, and the springboard from which he searches for another world, a less-material world. It is part of the *search for significance.* Perhaps this search, or drive, derives from the same causes that brought life into being in the first place and that set in process the vast evolutionary undertakings of nature. We cannot tell. An objective view is not possible to us, since a critical examination of the search would be one of its own manifestations.

When on occasion there comes common understanding, all too often the "common cause" turns out to be only a process whereby one group imposes its mores, rules, and outright control over the lives of others. The "cause" may originate from a specific situation or idea that grows and spreads by adopting a symbol, slogan, model, or idol that is appealing to the masses without being too demanding of logic or analysis. They grow even faster under umbrellas such as religion, nationalism, patriotism. Thereafter it is relatively easy to take advantage of social organizations to promulgate the cause to many people who for one reason or another give ready ear. The process represents a cybernetic system with positive feedback.

Examples of "cause" and growth processes such as these have been legion, including almost every religious movement, every demonstration of social conscience, and all the phenomena represented by the Bonapartes, Hitlers, Ku Klux Klan, Communism, the Civil Liberties Union, or the Society for the Prevention of Cruelty to Animals. Large or small, good or bad, they usually follow this path. The surprising and distressing aspect is not in the coming of new ideas but in the situation that organizations and institutions seem to provide pliable instrumentalities whereby to enslave people as easily as to benefit them. Thus widespread agreement among members of the community can be as harmful as widespread differences can be, as when the community as a whole develops intolerance toward a minority. The task for those who manage the affairs of a community is therefore not so much to unify as to co-ordinate and to make it possible for differences to exist and to complement each other. The co-ordination can extend to job activities and to the activities of churches, although here especially "one man's meat is another man's poison."

Social institutions as cybernetic systems

We wonder why organizations of people and their institutions are so pliable on some occasions and so inertia-laden for changes in other directions. The reasons are probably related to the uncertain foundations and purposes of society. Indeed much of the search is for these very foundations and purposes. Along with clinging to old patterns and values, there is awareness of the contradictions in those values. The awareness and the search are supported by a natural revulsion against sameness. For while the question "to be or not to be" poses a serious obstacle to drastic moves on the part of individuals, there is in every one of us also a willingness (if not outright demand) for change and for novelty.

The objectives and processes of a community are revealed not so much by the orators of the community as by the character of its institutions and institutional activities. The number and quality of the schools, museums, musical organizations, news media, theaters, research institutions, industrial firms, stores, churches, corrective institutions, forms of government, homes for the sick and the aged, etc., represent focal points for community interests and energies. Moreover, the community and the people themselves will be guided largely by the institutions they establish and maintain. For example, the schools that a community builds and the teachers it supports will also help to determine the trend of thinking of the future citizens of the community. An inbred situation leads to an excess of "negative feedback," which prevents growth or change, while a combination of negative feedback and receptivity to new ideas can provide stability and progress. The community is a living organism, and every institution within it performs a function, much as the individual parts of the body perform as living organs.

Since institutions represent the efforts of numbers of people, they also suffer the virtues and ills that are associated with large groups of people. For example, the existence of a large, representative governing body for the community means that legislative and executive functions are likely to assume large, mass properties, which prevent their reacting quickly. Even educational organizations, which by the nature of their interests might be expected to be quickly responsive to new knowledge or new social conditions or new methods of teaching and learning, are likely to become inertia-laden, unresponsive institutions. A group of innovative educators would become badly frustrated if they were to attempt to modernize school curriculums at a much faster rate than the community's awareness of the need for changes. A symphony orchestra leader who tries to be innovative may find that his contract is not renewed. The same can be said for most other kinds of institutions.

In other words, while, like a living organism, a community must accept change, its composition and size make for quite different possibilities for the changes that are acceptable. Against the easy exchanges that are possible in a family or in test-tube chemistry, the organization now experiences inertia, delays, and instabilities comparable to the characteristics of large chemical production plants (Fig. 33). Unfortunately it is much more difficult to prevent excessive fluctuations in a social system than it is in chemical plants. The delays, inertia, and cyclic oscillations of institutions and of communities can be tolerable except when they are motivated and energized by "causes" that convert mass momentum to mass hysteria or mob psychology.

Thus organizations and institutions bring a combination of gains and losses to the individual, with strong likelihood that an individual will find himself to be only an unhappy globule in a surging sea.

The cybernetic approach to urban situations

The well-being of a community is determined by a great variety of factors. Where farm products are involved there will be uncertain effects of seed quality, weather, availability of farm hands, size of harvest in relation to demand, competition, availability of other food supplies, etc. Where factories are involved the uncertain influences from other communities add to the confusion. There may be influences from the fashion experts, from tourism, from the effect of weather on resort areas, etc. The effects and influences multiply as people gather in urban centers. It is here especially that the *attitude* required by cybernetics discourages approaching situations like the proverbial "bull in a china shop," through awareness that feedback may be circuitous and in subtle forms.

At this writing the large urban centers are quite distressed over their economic plight and the problem of eliminating slum districts. "Housing for the poor" has become an important political and social issue, and some cities have undertaken major programs for replacing slum areas with large investments in apartment buildings. The results have been far from successful, however, for as pointed out by Forrester* the benefits of new housing or of jobs for the unemployed may easily disappear with rapid influx of more jobless into the city. And according to Forrester the rate at which the underemployed move into a city is determined by thirty-one feedback influences, some of which are indicated in Fig. 34. The models he developed representing urban situations as systems, made extensive use of computers and feedback loops of many kinds. In one model, housing was constructed each year in sufficient numbers to

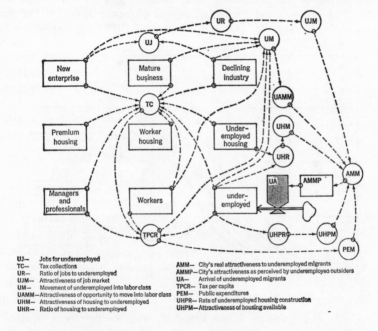

UJ— Jobs for underemployed
TC— Tax collections
UR— Ratio of jobs to underemployed
UJM— Attractiveness of job market
UM— Movement of underemployed into labor class
UAMM—Attractiveness of opportunity to move into labor class
UHM— Attractiveness of housing to underemployed
UHR— Ratio of housing to underemployed

AMM— City's real attractiveness to underemployed migrants
AMMP—City's attractiveness as perceived by underemployed outsiders
UA— Arrival of underemployed migrants
TPCR— Tax per capita
PEM— Public expenditures
UHPR— Rate of underemployed housing construction
UHPM—Attractiveness of housing available

Fig. 34. Forrester's findings on the complex factors that influence the arrival of underemployed migrants. (Courtesy of The M.I.T. Press)

*Jay W. Forrester, *Urban Dynamics* (Cambridge, Mass.: The M.I.T. Press, 1969).

202

care for 5% of the unemployed of each year. The conclusion of a fifty-year period seemed to show not solution of the problem but denser slums, fewer jobs for the underemployed, a drop of 30% in the population of skilled workers, and even larger drops in new and old business establishments. The causes seemed to be excessive influx of unemployed into the city and deteriorating incentives for attracting new business activities of the right kind.

Forrester's conclusions seemed to be that the computer and the systems representation of urban situations are both necessary and effective. Also, there are available abundant data with which to analyze real situations, the more serious problem being appreciation of the subtle interrelationships that exist in each situation—interrelationships that often cross disciplinary boundaries into the intangible realms of the psychology of a community. Figure 34 illustrates some of the unusual interrelationships Forrester found to be important, and Fig. 35 the results of analysis of an urban model

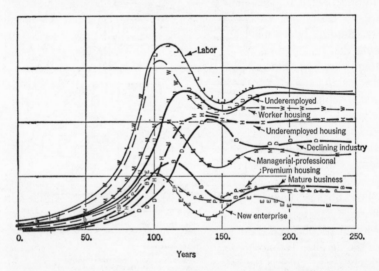

Fig. 35. The Forrester urban model involves mathematical equations stored in a computer. He inserted in the equations data representing the condition of a hypothetical city at its birth. The computer then produced the above chart showing the city's growth and stagnation over a 250-year period. Mr. Forrester says the general long-term relationships hold, despite short-term fluctuations caused by technological innovations and world events. (Courtesy of The M.I.T. Press)

over a 250-year period. Note that the curves of the latter figure have the same general features that were observed for the damped oscillating system with negative feedback (curve 1 of Fig. 5). One criticism that might be made of his conclusions arises from the need to apply such studies on a regional or national scale, since the influx of unemployed into one area may represent a different kind of change in the area from which they come.

Science, technology, and Social purpose

The problems of this generation reach beyond urban dynamics, however. The decade of the 1970s finds the world in a mood that is uncommonly subdued, concerned, and even fearful, the concern being shared as much by the man in the street as by governments around the world. The causes for concern include old problems that go under the names of poverty, ghettos, hunger, race relations, social injustice, struggling minorities, inadequate governments, and political ideologies that "liberate" people by destroying their individuality. But the issues have assumed such dangerous proportions that both the thinking and the unthinking worlds want to know the reasons why. The "reasons why" involve not only political and social leadership, but also science, engineering, education, and industry, which for many years have been regarded as creators of progress. Scientists and engineers were the fair-haired boys who discovered how to exploit the energy resources of nature to make them servants of mankind. They made possible abundant food supplies, comfort, conveniences, fast travel, medical services, and many other goodies. Conditions changed, however. Along with the goodies there came nuclear bombs in larger and larger numbers. Education through college levels became available to vast numbers of students without producing corresponding responsiveness to the critical needs of the decade. Technological industry and the gross national product reached new heights but left the poor even poorer. The technology that made for convenience and abundance turned to pollute and despoil nature itself. And out of this mix of sociotechnological, socioeconomic, and political contradictions, there came erosion of family life along with frustration among the young, and rebellion.

These certainly were not the results that were intended by scientists and technologists, any more than it was intended by educators, sociologists, and politicians that we should continue to have only bad or inadequate governments and poverty around the world. It seems clear that we, meaning mankind and society as a whole, are midstream in evolutionary changes, and that science and technology are especially in a stage of rapid transition. Midstream or not, however, we have arrived at a point of history that demands careful evaluation of where we are headed, and what the roles of technology and of education are to be. The pressure is on for society as a whole to demonstrate sensitivity and responsiveness to the long-range consequences of its many doings. As one aspect of this pressure, scientists and technologists may no longer accept the role of hirelings with minimal interest in the objectives or uses of their output. In short, the times demand maturing and a sense of purpose by all of society.

The task is not to bury civilization or technology in a wave of pessimism, but to determine what changes are called for that promote the over-all and especially the long-range viability of man. Science and technology and education simply extend the capabilities that arms and legs and brains provide, and as such are inherently good or bad in the same way that our body capabilities are inherently good or bad. The body performs for good or for ill strictly as determined by mental processes, and science and technology similarly are guided by individual and collective attitudes and decisions of society. We note, however, that just as the movements of the infant body are unco-ordinated and useless, and become useful only through achievement of co-ordination, maturity, and purpose, so science and technology also require a learning period, self-discipline, maturity, and a sense of purpose. We have had one form of self-discipline within science, the kind that permits individual experiments to be successful, but *self-discipline with a larger social purpose has yet to come.*

We recall that when science had its beginnings in the post-Renaissance period it was necessary to tear away the strangle hold on new ideas that had worked its way into religious dogma. It was imperative that the search for the laws of nature be pursued without depending on the dictates of the Church and without ascribing a principal role to deity for the day-by-day management of the universe. The workings of the human body and of the mind had to be studied "objectively," with the idea that they could be explained in terms of mechanistic principles that were even then just being revealed. However, in the process of becoming "objective," science also became essentially purposeless as far as moral or social goals were concerned. The emphasis was to be on science for the sake of knowledge—nothing else.

The spirit of the time was expressed by Lord Kelvin's thesis to the effect that only through measurements and numbers may one have understanding that is better than the "meager and unsatisfactory kind." The attitude encouraged physical scientists to exclude from their domain nearly all phenomena, including philosophic thinking, that were not reducible to quantitative measurements. Since human emotions do not permit precise measurement, the "scientific" posture excluded the most significant features of living experiences. Recent decades have softened the attitude to permit recognition of the behavioral sciences, but the attitude is still more of tolerance than of acceptance to full partnership with these fields.

While this overaddiction to the Kelvin thesis encouraged rapid progress in the physical sciences, success has been far from complete. For example, despite all the exact equations and precise data that revolve around gravitational attraction, we still are as uninformed as ever on the basic *causes* of this most common and general property of matter. In comparison, consider the simple experience of a person striking another person: the original act and the mental and physical response from the struck individual are so complex as to be beyond measurement, yet there is probably more comprehension of *why* the struck individual strikes back (or fails to strike back) than accompanies our understanding of gravitational attraction. Nevertheless numbers and equations are so useful that engineering and science students turn to them as quickly as possible. Only the uncommon teacher explores with a science class the quandaries of action at a distance, the "why" of electricity, the strangeness of the quantum conditions that govern atomic structure, or why entropy changes in living systems have reverse direction. Only by concentrating on numbers and equations to the exclusion of more-penetrating questions and unknowns do these disciplines have the appearance of being "exact sciences."

The historical reasons for the condition are fairly clear. Without expecting to become a factor in the socioeconomic world, science gave birth to the Industrial Revolution and has been supporting its growth ever since. As the relationship between science and technology became more direct, most of the scientists themselves became hirelings to the industrial complex. From the singleness of purpose implied in the phrase "science for the sake of knowledge" it was an easy step to science for the sake of industrial progress and profit. Unfortunately this left little room for concern over long-range effects on the generations yet to come.

The challenge for today

In our own day, profit motives and short-range goals continue to dominate the technological/industrial military complex, and only public pressure expressed through governmental agencies prevents wholesale damage to public interests. Meanwhile we have entered the *computer age,* with capabilities and sophistication that exceed any achieved to date. In the absence of clearer social objectives, however, the additional capabilities give only "more of the same," to add to the confusion on what constitute social justice and social stability or to add to the waste and rape of natural resources.

A cybernetic "analysis" of any socioeconomic system quickly brings the realization that the "system" includes more than science and technology, more than governmental authority, and more than the capabilities of single communities working alone. Moreover, while every region has problems that encompass energy availability, public health, food, and all the accompaniments of urban living and social change, the situations are far from being similar as one goes from continent to continent. Although a world view is imperative for the reason that the problems of pollution, disease, and hunger of one region cannot be isolated from those of other regions, each region must find its own, differing answers to questions of rate of materials and energy utilization, population limits, standard of living, etc. Each will also find different answers concerning its responsibility to generations yet to come. Within each continent, however, there are conflicting interests between major segments of society. For example, while scientists and technologists can discover guidelines and alternatives for waste management, energy utilization, urban and transportation facilities, public health, and stable ecological relationships with respect to population size and regional resources, the decisions on what will be done remain with a variety of competitive taxpayers and segments of society.

For these reasons the well-being of the generations to come places a rather heavy burden on educational institutions, for they are the principal media through which the attitudes that govern the future are formed. That is, when viewed in the framework of cybernetic systems, the effectiveness of controls is determined by the *adequacy of the informational elements* of the system. The burden falls first on the colleges and universities, where the teachers of the lower grades have their own preparation.

Presumably, placing the burden on universities should give comfort to society, for educators are expected to be sources for both new knowledge and interpretation of its significance. That new knowledge originates in educational institutions is indeed true, but the interpretive processes are severely faulty. The faculties and curriculums that prepare attorneys, businessmen, government leaders, economists, sociologists, anthropologists, physicists, chemists, biologists, etc., are ensconced in their own intellectual cubbyholes. Over the years each has developed a scope of interests that makes too little room for interests lying outside that scope. With few exceptions the parochialism this has engendered under the name of specialization stands in the way of relating to each other or to the larger issues of nature and of society. Chasms exist not only between the sciences and the humanities, but also among the disciplines that make up the sciences and among the disciplines that carry the general title of humanities. The latter have been especially negligent about providing guidance for directing the uses of science and technology.

The most important first steps toward improvement must come from college and university departments—from restudy of what constitutes well-rounded education for our present world, and relaxation from the rigidity that presently characterizes most curriculums. The greater flexibility must also be extended to the secondary schools and to the examinations that students must pass in order to be rated by state education departments or by the colleges. The examinations have been "straitjackets" from decades that have long receded into the crevices of history.

There are other handicaps as well. Too many college curriculums are made suitable for students who would do better in vocational schools. Professional societies tend to impose their own image on each new generation. The universities are handicapped by large proportions of tenure faculty who stand in the way of new courses

and new curriculums. Government agencies that support research
are administered by people who are either too fearful of sponsoring
innovations in education or are held back from doing so by college
professors who act as reviewers and referees on proposals. Respectable professional journals remain respectable by assiduously avoid-
ing departures from the conventional in the articles they accept for
publication.

The handicaps reduce progress to a crawl, but there is progress,
nevertheless. In time, not only will educational institutions respond
to changing needs but so will the other professional and non-profes-
sional elements that control our world. This represents an optimistic
view, with full recognition that evolutionary processes can destroy
as easily as build up. The pressures that are being applied at this
writing by idealistic youth against social mores, educational institutions, social conscience, and governmental "defense" posture represent a considerable asset of the moment; but the asset can disappear
if the more informed generation does not respond and guide the way
toward more-meaningful social goals.*

In conclusion

What shall we say as to the usefulness of cybernetics for revealing the secrets of natural processes? It is clear that while the presence in an organism of negative-feedback loops and of positive-
feedback loops helps to explain many functional characteristics of
organisms, they alone do not reveal the internal "drive" that motivates organismic growth. Nor is there adequate understanding of
how natural fluctuations and positive feedback find transition to
negative feedback that introduces equilibrium and a stable state. To
be sure, cybernetic systems are goal-oriented, and the "goals" or
drives may have much to do with this transformation from one
stable state to another.

The picture is incomplete and becomes more so when we probe
man's search for meaning in the universe and man's concern with
the future. Teilhard de Chardin refers to evolution as having "precise *orientation* and a privileged axis." Some would picture man's
evolution as perhaps being the most "privileged" and possibly en-

---

* See *A Systems Analysis of Political Life,* by David Easton (New York: John
Wiley, 1965).

dowed with its own internal genetic endowment toward predetermined goals (orthogenesis).

These, then, constitute some of the features of "this cybernetic world." On the one hand there are the forces that maintain sameness in the physical and biological world and guides that, like the Ten Commandments, decree what shall not be done. But novelty does on occasion "insinuate" itself into this sameness, and lo! new phenomena come into being within the framework of "sameness." In place of "an eye for an eye" there suddenly appears the plea to "Do good to them that hate you," and the world is no longer quite the same. And yet it is the same, for the cybernetic world is a dynamic world, a changing world with "purposes" and goals and processes that have yet to be revealed.

References

ASHBY, W. ROSS, *An Introduction to Cybernetics* (London: Chapman and Hall, 1961).

BERNARD, CLAUDE, *Introduction to the Study of Experimental Medicine* (New York: Macmillan, 1957). First published in 1865.

BRILLOUIN, L., *Science and Information Theory* (New York: Academic Press, 1956).

BUCKLEY, WALTER, ed., *Modern Systems Research for the Behavioral Scientist* (Chicago: Aldine Publishing Co., 1968). A source book for the application of general systems theory to the study of human behavior.

CORNING, WILLIAM C. and MARTIN BALABAN, *The Mind: Biological Approaches to Its Functions* (New York: Wiley [Interscience], 1968).

CROSSON, F. J. and SAYRE, K. M., ed., *Philosophy and Cybernetics* (New York: Simon & Schuster, 1968). A Clarion Book paperback on information theory.

ELLIS, WILLIS D., *A Source Book of Gestalt Psychology* (New York: Humanities Press, 1967). This book contains chapters by Max Wertheimer and by others who have been leaders in this approach to psychology.

FOX, SIDNEY W., ed., *The Origins of Prebiological Systems and Their Molecular Matrices* (New York: Academic Press, 1965).

HARTLEY, R. V. L., "Transmission of Information," *Bell System Tech. J.* 7, 1928.

MCCULLOCH, W. S. and W. PITTS, "A Logical Calculus of the Ideas Immanent in Nervous Activity," *Bull. Math. Biophys.*, 5, 1943, p. 115, and 9, 1947, p. 127.

MCCULLOCH, WARREN S., *Embodiment of Mind* (Cambridge, Mass.: The M.I.T. Press, 1965).

MILLER, S. L., "A Production of Amino Acids Under Possible Primitive Earth Conditions," *Science* 117, 528, 1953.

OPARIN, A. I., *The Origin of Life* (a translation with annotations by S. Morgulis) (New York: Macmillan, 1938).

PARSEGIAN, V. L., A. S. MELTZER, K. S. KINERSON, A. S. LUCHINS, *Introduc-*

tion to Natural Science, Part I—The Physical Sciences (New York: Academic Press, 1968).

PARSEGIAN, V. L., F. V. MONAGHAN, P. R. SHILLING, A. S. LUCHINS, *Introduction to Natural Science,* Part II—The Life Sciences (New York: Academic Press, 1970).

PARSEGIAN, V. L., *Toward a Viable Future for Man* (Scranton, Pa.: International Text Co., 1972). (An introduction to environmental-ecological and socioeconomic stresses.)

QUARTON, GARDNER C., THEODORE MELNECHUK, FRANCIS O. SCHMITT, *The Neurosciences: A Study Program* (New York: The Rockefeller University Press, 1967).

QUASTLER, HENRY, *The Emergence of Biological Organization* (New Haven, Conn.: Yale University Press, 1964).

RANDALL, JAMES E., *Elements of Biophysics,* 2d Ed. (Chicago: Year Book Medical Publishers, 1962).

SHANNON, C. E. and W. WEAVER, *The Mathematical Theory of Communication* (Urbana, Ill.: Univ. of Illinois Press, 1949).

SILLIMAN, R. P. and J. S. GUTSELL, "Experimental Exploitation of Fish Populations," *U. S. Fish and Wildlife Service Bulletin* 58, 1958.

SINGH, JAGJIT, *Great Ideas in Information Theory, Language and Cybernetics* (New York: Dover Publications, 1966).

UREY, H., *The Planets, Their Origin and Development* (New Haven, Conn.: Yale University Press, 1952).

WHITEHEAD, ALFRED NORTH, *The Function of Reason* (Boston, Mass.: Beacon Press). This very thoughtful little volume comprises three lectures delivered at Princeton University in 1929. It was republished in 1958 as a First Beacon Paperback edition.

WIENER, NORBERT, *Cybernetics* (New York: John Wiley & Sons, Inc., and Cambridge, Mass.: The M.I.T. Press, 2d Ed., 1961).

WYBURN, G. M., R. W. PICKFORD, and R. J. HIRST, *Human Senses and Perception* (Toronto: Univ. of Toronto Press, 1964).

WYNNE-EDWARDS, V. C., "Self-regulating Systems in Populations of Animals," *Science* 147, 1543ff., 1965.